Shade Gardening
with
Derek Fell

Shade Gardening

with

Derek Fell

*Practical Advice and
Personal Favorites
from the Best-Selling Author
and Television Show Host*

FRIEDMAN/FAIRFAX
PUBLISHERS

A FRIEDMAN/FAIRFAX BOOK

© 1998 by Michael Friedman Publishing Group, Inc.

Library of Congress Cataloging-in-Publication data available upon request

ISBN 1-56799-707-4

Editors: Susan Lauzau and Penelope O'Sullivan
Art Director: Jeff Batzli
Designer: Jennifer Markson
Photography Director: Christopher C. Bain
Production Manager: Camille Lee

Color separations by Colourscan Overseas Co Pte Ltd
Printed in Singapore by Tien Wah Press (PTE) Limited

10   9   8   7   6   5   4   3   2   1

For bulk purchases and special sales, please contact:
Friedman/Fairfax Publishers
Attention: Sales Department
15 West 26th Street
New York, New York 10010
212/685-6610   FAX 212/685-1307

Visit our website:
http://www.metrobooks.com

Frontispiece: A dense planting of ostrich ferns and rhododendrons makes this woodland garden lush and lovely.

Dedication

For my three children, Christina, Victoria, and Derek Jr.,
all of whom love gardening.

Acknowledgments

There are many fine gardeners whom I must thank for inviting me into their shady sanctuaries and for giving me the opportunity to capture their innovative gardens on film. They provided a wealth of inspiration and ideas that helped me plan and plant the ambitious shade garden at my own home, Cedaridge Farm, in beautiful Bucks County, Pennsylvania.

Although some of these expert shade gardeners live in other countries, their ideas translate very well to North America. First, I thank Princess Greta Sturdza, owner of Le Vasterival, a magnificent woodland garden on the Normandy coast. In a pocket of acid soil along a wooded ravine, she has established a world-class garden. Shade-tolerant plants in a symphony of color harmonies and structural accents make the garden at Le Vasterival a visual pleasure in any season.

Closer to home is Jack Miller, a moss garden expert who established a tranquil environment full of soothing influences on a small wooded slope near Collegeville, Pennsylvania. Ted Neiremberg, founder of Dansk Dinnerware, cultivates a dramatic woodland garden near Mt. Kisco in New York State. His garden encompasses beautiful lakeside vistas and rock gardens colonized by wildflowers among groves of native white birch, maple, and shadblow trees that reach a crescendo of color in autumn. I also owe my keen appreciation of shade gardens to J. Drayton Hastie, owner of Magnolia Plantation in South Carolina. His garden is in a swamp, shaded by tall cypress trees garlanded with Spanish moss. Hastie maintains four seasons of color in his garden, despite savage summer heat. I am indebted to Colin Spicer, a New Zealand gardener who single-handedly maintains what I consider to be the most magical shade garden I have ever seen, using plants in bold brush strokes of color along a woodland stream in a design that makes the entire landscape appear perfectly natural.

There is a little of these gardens on my own property, including a swamp garden, stream garden, and woodland wildflower garden. The ideas expressed in this book, therefore, are all tested and true. None of these plantings, however, would have been possible without the help of my grounds supervisor, Wendy Fields, and my wife, Carolyn. Thanks also to Kathy Nelson, my office manager, who helps to keep my extensive photo library organized.

Opposite: This formal garden at Magnolia Plantation in South Carolina features plants associated with the Bible.

The garden is made more charming by its setting within a woodland clearing.

Introduction

This tapestry garden at Cedaridge Farm is framed by a fringe of shadowy trees and plants. Rather than focusing on color, tapestry gardens rely on the rich composition of foliage effects for visual interest.

Although many of us love to bask in the sun and need sunshine for our well-being, shade is a welcome respite. It soothes our souls, and of course, its cooling influence brings some relief from summer's heat.

But what is shade? This may seem like a rhetorical question, but the term requires accurate definition. In the gardening world, any site that receives less than six hours of direct sunlight is considered shady. Yet experiments with light at the University of North Carolina show that as little as a 1 percent difference in light intensity can make a 100 percent difference in plant growth. This is the difference between flowers and no flowers at all.

Take my own garden, for example—a property that encompasses 24 acres (9.6ha) of sloping ground, a third of which is wooded. Often, the removal of a single tree limb makes the difference between a plant struggling for survival and profuse flowering.

Similarly, the reflective quality of an adjacent wall or fence can make such a huge difference that most of our garden structures in shady areas (gazebos, arbors, barns, and toolsheds) are painted white.

When people visit my garden, their tour generally begins at a path that meanders along the edge of a wildflower meadow flooded in sunlight. Corn poppies, ox-eye daisies, and bachelor's buttons gleam like jewels among native grasses. A rose arch announces the entrance to the cultivated garden, where on hot sunny days visitors are relieved to see that the path leads to a corner of deeply shaded woodland. On the woodland floor grow blue hostas, silver ferns, bright green cushions of moss, and lustrous evergreen hellebores, planted for contrasting leaf shapes, textures, and colors. The path then leads through a grove of native wild plum, which creates a canopy of fragrant white blossoms in spring. An elevated wooden bridge and a boardwalk over a stream conduct visitors to a lightly shaded bog garden, planted generously with primulas and flag irises. Through the bog garden, the path enters another heavily shaded area, which

For a grassy path that meanders through shady areas, it is best to plant shade-tolerant lawn fescue. Here the verdant grass path curves below a slope planted with azaleas.

I describe as a leaf tunnel. Branches of tall maples arch high overhead, creating a cathedral of cool green tones in spring and golden hues in autumn. Because of the high canopy, just enough dappled light penetrates the leaves for fescue to create a grassy path, for azaleas and rhododendrons to flower along a slope, and for wildflowers to generously colonize the edges. Our visitors emerge from the winding leaf tunnel into an oasis of light. The path continues along sunny lawn vistas to traditional cutting gardens, cottage gardens, vegetable gardens, and perennial borders. It then doubles back and returns to the rose arch along a shadier route.

Many kinds of shade exist in my garden, from light shade, where some sun-loving plants can thrive, to deep shade, where little more than mosses, ferns, and ivy feel comfortable. Other kinds of shade include dry and moist shade, low and high shade, exposed and sheltered shade, and morning, noon, and afternoon shade. The kind of shade influences the type of plant that will grow in a garden.

In addition to light intensity, soil quality and air circulation also affect a shade garden. Indeed, most plants noted for growing well in shade will perform poorly if the soil is dry or shallow. This is particularly true of shade-loving annuals such as impatiens, which demand a deep, humus-rich, moisture-retentive soil. Where soil is shallow or dry (compacted clay soils are particularly bad), the best course of action is to make a raised bed using tree limbs or stones. Do

Above: A flagstone path traverses a shady bulb garden. Below: Rough stones create a dramatic change of elevation in a Japanese garden.

not disturb the compacted soil if there are tree roots near the surface, since disturbing these feeder roots may harm the tree. Instead, bring in some good topsoil or garden compost to make a planting space above the compacted area.

Many plants recommended for shade, such as primulas and garden lilies, can rot in a poorly ventilated space, especially where tree branches sweep low over them or where dense shrubs like azaleas are planted too close. Each spring, when deciduous trees start to unfurl their leaves, I take a critical look at their placement and prune away all branches that exceed their bounds or intrude into susceptible plantings, taking care to maintain some protective shelter from searing winds and freezing cold.

Although the selection of plants for shade gardens is not as broad as for sunny ones, the potential for creativity is greater because visual interest on a shady site can extend for a considerable height. Floor-to-ceiling interest is possible not only by choosing trees with sculptural forms, but also by selecting suitable shrubs, vines, and groundcovers. Shade gardens have at least three levels of dramatic interest—the floor, the understory, and the leaf canopy. Even a site shaded by a tall building or a high wall can be worked into a three-level design that infuses the entire field of vision with beauty.

For the past thirty years, I have photographed every kind of landscaped garden, including many of the world's best shade gardens. I also spent seven years creating a satisfying series of shade gardens at my home, where nothing but brambles and poison ivy had previously grown. These gardens have been featured in *Architectural Digest, American Nurseryman, Fine Gardening,* and *Beautiful Gardens,* as well as in magazines such as *Garden Illustrated* (U.K.), *The Journal of the Royal Horticultural Society* (U.K.), and *The New Zealand Gardener.*

Graceful Grecian-style columns with wood crossbeams help to create a romantic shady path that connects two sunny garden spaces.

Large trees, judiciously pruned, inscribe beautiful shadow patterns across the lawn in the early morning and late afternoon.

Although my wife and I designed some of our shade gardens under existing trees or beside shady walls, our most impressive shade gardens have been made from scratch—planting fast-growing trees like 'Heritage' river birch and dawn redwood to create shade where none previously existed. Our gardens also contain arches, arbors, and pergolas festooned with morning glories, trumpet vines, and clematis to break the fierce heat of the sun and create "instant" shade for low-growing plants such as violets, impatiens, and hostas.

One benefit of a shade garden is the minimum of care required for its upkeep. Growth rates are slow, weed seeds germinate poorly, and pests and diseases are fewer in the shade. Plants require less water because soil moisture evaporates slowly, and plant losses from exposure to wind and cold are fewer than in full sun. Once a shade garden is in place, it is relatively easy to maintain, especially with weed-suffocating mulches like shredded leaves and dense evergreen groundcovers like hostas and ivy.

Moreover, certain design elements look better in shade than they do in full sun. For example, tapestry effects involving contrasts of foliage can look sensational in a shady setting, while harsh sunlight saturates gradations of green and causes some of the best leaf forms like hostas and ferns to wilt or burn.

Pools, fountains, benches, bridges, stepping-stones, and paths also look better in shade, especially dappled shade, where light and shadow can create beautiful patterns. Water in particular should be a prime consideration when creating a shade garden. The sound of water is nature's music, resonant in shade and attractive to songbirds. Reflections in water double the beauty of their surroundings. If you do not have a gurgling stream or a glittering pond, then consider creating a small, fern-fringed pool.

In this book, I strive to elevate shade gardens above the mundane, to produce not only a pleasant escape from summer's heat but also a visual thrill, no matter what the season or time of day.

Blue flowers, such as these forget-me-nots, are especially beautiful for edging shady paths.

Identifying Different Types of Shade

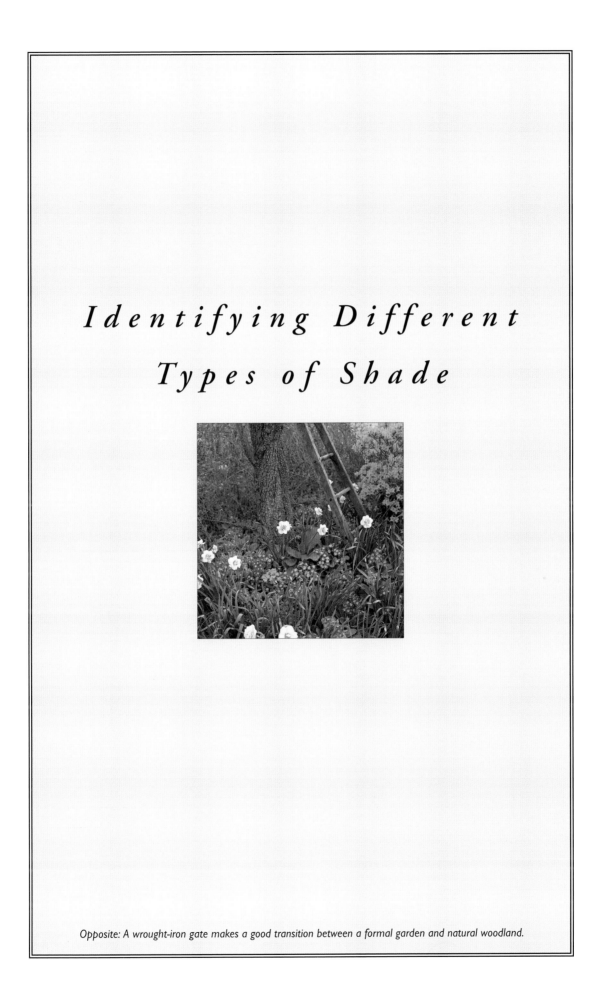

Identifying Different Types of Shade

The overhead leaf canopy along this woodland path, which is edged with blue phlox, tulips, and perennial yellow alyssum, is thinned regularly to maintain dappled shade.

Most gardening reference books refer to sites with fewer than six hours of direct sunlight as shady, depending on the time of day those six hours of sunlight occur. If those six hours occur in the middle of the day then the site can safely be considered sunny, but if the six hours are all at the beginning or end of the day, then six hours may be insufficient for many sun-loving plants such as melons and sunflowers. Morning light is more important than afternoon light, because reddish tones from infrared rays infuse sun rays in the afternoon.

Sometimes, however, it is not shade that allows a shade-loving plant to grow well but rather the presence of cool, moist soil, which shade encourages. Impatiens, wax begonias, and coleus are popular shade-loving plants that thrive in full sun, provided the soil stays cool and moist by mulching and irrigation. In

Color Harmonies for Shade

The best shade gardens play the color keyboard to present symphonies of colors that look good together. By studying a color wheel you can see that colors close to each other (like pink and blue, or orange and yellow) are good to combine, as are colors opposite each other (like red and green, yellow and violet, or orange and blue). Monochromatic color combinations are also effective in shade gardens, especially shades of blue and the many gradations of white, (such as cream, gray, and silver), which can produce a glittering effect if sprinkled about and not clumped tightly together. However, for the strongest dramatic impact using one color, make it red. The complement of red is green, and since shade gardens already have plenty of green, all you need for a good show are plants with red hues. Astilbes, azaleas, begonias, bleeding heart, caladiums, camellias, cardinal flower, coleus, foxgloves, impatiens, lilies, primulas, rhododendrons, scarlet sage, and berry bushes such as skimmia, viburnums, and winterberry can all provide different shades of red. The pink and blue color harmony shown below was created with pink azaleas and bluebells.

southern states and desert areas, intense summer heat can make growing many sun-loving plants impossible. Plants need the presence of light shade, from live oak trees for example, to prevent their burning in the high heat.

Seasonal shade is also a vital consideration. Daffodils adorn deciduous woodlands in early spring before the tree leaves unfurl. Because sunshine can reach the earth through the leafless branches, daffodil foliage receives enough light to recharge the bulb. In evergreen woodlands, where shady conditions persist during the blooming period and during bulb regeneration, weak growth will result, and the planting will gradually peter out from lack of light.

To simplify the subject, gardeners identify the three main types of shade as light shade, medium shade, and deep shade. When you look at a plant label or catalog description, you will often see a circle that is one-third black or all gray representing a plant that tolerates light shade, a half-black circle for medium shade, and an all-black circle for deep shade. A clear circle means the plant requires full sun (usually a minimum of six hours.)

The waterfall in this backyard woodland garden is man-made, using a pump to recirculate the water. Billowing dogwoods carry color high above the woodland floor while upright ostrich ferns and hemlocks add structural interest to the understory.

A Japanese maple clothed in autumn colors is backlit by the sun.

Seasonal Shade Gardens

Much of North America has snow cover or freezing temperatures in winter, which encourages spectacular fall coloring. At a time when sunny gardens are exhausting themselves and flowering poorly, shade gardens can finish the season with a flourish of intense reds, golds, oranges, and yellows derived from woody plants noted for splendid color changes. Following is a list of small hardy trees and shrubs known for their spectacular autumn color:

Acer palmatum (Japanese maple tree)—red and orange

Amelanchier canadensis (serviceberry tree)—yellow and orange

Aronia arbutifolia (chokeberry shrub)—red

Betula nigra (river birch tree)—yellow

Betula papyrifera (white birch tree)—yellow and lime green

Calycanthus floridus (sweet shrub)—yellow

Cornus floridus (dogwood tree)—red and purple

Enkianthus campanulatus (bellflower shrub)—orange and red

Euonymus alatus (burning bush)—red and pink

Fothergilla major (fothergilla shrub)—orange

Hamamelis mollis (witch hazel tree)—orange

Oxydendrum arboreum (sourwood tree)—orange

Rhus typhina (staghorn sumac tree)—red and orange

Plants That Tolerate Light Shade

Some outstanding plants for light shade include the following:

Acanthus mollis (bear's breeches)

Alchemilla mollis (lady's mantle)

Anemone nemerosa (wood anemone)

Astilbe × arendsii (false goatsbeard, false spirea)

Corydalis flexuosa (blue bleeding heart)

Cyclamen hederifolium (ivy-leaf cyclamen)

Digitalis purpurea (common foxglove)

Eranthis hyemalis (winter aconite)

Fritillaria imperialis (crown imperial)

Hemerocallis hybrids (daylilies)

Iris cristata (crested iris)

Kerria japonica (Japanese kerria)

Lilium 'Asiatic hybrids' (Asiatic lilies)

Lobelia cardinalis (cardinal flower)

Lunaria annua (money plant)

Mertensia virginica (Virginia bluebell)

Myosotis alpestris (forget-me-not)

Narcissus hybrids (daffodils)

Paeonia officinalis (peony)

Rhododendron hybrids (azaleas)

Scilla hispanica [Endymion hispanicus, Hyacinthoides hispanica] (Spanish bluebell)

Tulipa hybrids (tulips)

Mixed varieties of pansies create a colorful floral carpet in a lightly shaded Victorian-style garden.

Light Shade

Light shade is sometimes described as partial shade. A site shaded all morning, at noon, or all afternoon can produce light shade. Light shade can also come from a high canopy, such as tall trees with fine leaves or a building permanently shading a site. The latter must allow a fair amount of light to filter from the sides, an effect that can be magnified by painting the wall surface white to increase light reflectiveness. The rule of thumb is that if turf grass (especially fescue) is growing on a shady site, then the site has light shade. This test is particularly helpful in classifying shade from trees, since some, like mimosas, have the feathery leaves and wide-spreading branches that allow good light penetration while others, like rhododendrons and oaks, can effectively block light.

The formal pool at Winterthur Garden in Delaware contrasts sharply with its informal setting. The landscape is especially alluring in spring when the dogwood trees are in full bloom.

Medium Shade

Medium shade is often referred to as half shade, and it is probably the shade condition we most encounter. If a site is in half shade, the sun doesn't linger long enough for it to be classified as lightly shaded, particularly when it is shaded for an extended period during the noon hours. I also classify the east side of a house foundation as having light shade and the west side as having medium shade, because morning light is more important than afternoon light. If, however, the east or west side of the house is also shaded by trees in addition to the wall, then this tends to produce deep shade. Medium shade is what we generally encounter in a deciduous woodland with a high leaf canopy. The movement of the sun across the leaves and the gentle movement of leaves from wind produces dappled light and shadow patterns across the ground.

Deep Shade

Deep shade, also known as heavy shade or dark shade, is the most difficult shade condition of all for growing plants. Deep shade usually indicates a gloomy place with little or no direct sunlight at all. It is the domain of foliage plants, since the majority of ornamental flowering plants find deep shade intolerable. A heavy canopy from evergreen trees—especially pines and similar conifers with dark, densely knit leaves—

Large flowers, abundant bloom, and decorative foliage make 'Tango' impatiens a popular annual for deep shade.

Plants That Tolerate Medium Shade

Some excellent plants for medium shade include the following:

Aquilegia canadensis (wild columbine)

Begonia × *tuberhybrida* (tuberous begonia)

Camellia japonica (Japanese camellia)

Chrysogonum virginianum (goldenstar)

Clivia miniata (Kruger lily)

Coleus blumei (flame nettle)

Dicentra spectabilis (common bleeding heart)

Doronicum cordatum (leopard's-bane)

Hakonechloa macra (hakone grass)

Helleborus orientalis (Lenten rose)

Hesperis matronalis (dame's rocket)

Hydrangea macrophylla (French hydrangea)

Leucothoe fontanesiana (drooping leucothoe)

Ligularia stenocephala (ragwort)

Phlox stolonifera (creeping phlox)

Primula × *polyantha* (primrose)

Pulmonaria saccharata (lungwort)

Tiarella cordifolia (foamflower)

Viola odorata (sweet violet)

These orange- and yellow-flowered deciduous azaleas—all native to the Appalachian Mountains of North America—are highly fragrant.

can cause deep shade. It can also develop from closely spaced deciduous trees with large, overlapping leaves, such as oaks, hickories, and maples.

One of the best garden structures for a woodland is a gazebo that can double as a shelter from sudden downpours.

Two shading elements on one site may combine to create deep shade. For example, when shade is produced by both a high, dark wall and an overhanging tree, deep shade may result. Since removing the wall would be more difficult, removal of the tree can change the site into a medium-shaded location.

A sheltered location with low shadowy elements such as small trees and tall shrubs may also cause deep shade. This happens in courtyards and atriums, where the four sides of a building may block light from the sides and where small umbrella-shaped trees such as star magnolias or ornamental crabapples rob the floor of the limited amount of sunlight coming from above.

Few flowering plants will tolerate a deeply shaded location. The most successful results usually come from foliage plants with colorful leaves such as blue hostas, red caladiums, and silvery ferns. Yet removing a single tree branch, painting a dark wall white, or laying down a mulch of white landscape chips can change a deeply shaded location into a half-shaded site and encourage the flowering of impatiens, the most shade-tolerant of all flowering plants. For a deeply shaded site with low shade, removing all low branches would increase both the light penetration and the amount of air circulation.

Plants That Tolerate Deep Shade

Good plants for deep shade include the following:

Adiantum pedatum (maidenhair fern)

Aegopodium podagraria (bishop's weed)

Ajuga reptans (bugleweed)

Asarum europaeum (European ginger)

Bergenia cordifolia (heartleaf)

Caladium × *hortulanum* (rainbow plant)

Galium odoratum (sweet woodruff)

Hedera helix (English ivy)

Hosta hybrids (plantain lilies)

Impatiens wallerana (patience plant)

Lamium galeobdolon (yellow archangel)

Trillium chloropetalum (western trillium)

Vinca minor (periwinkle)

Dogwood trees and rhododendrons make excellent companions on this wooded slope.

Growing and Propagating Shade Plants

Opposite: Daffodil, tulip, and bluebell bulbs will flower in spring, making lovely partners for the existing shade-loving hellebores.

Buying plants ready-grown can be expensive, but it is often easy to propagate your own from seed, division, or cuttings. Most annuals like impatiens and coleus are easily raised from seed. While most perennials are easily increased by division, many can also be raised from seed, and

Evergreen, grasslike lilyturf makes a good weed-suffocating groundcover for shady slopes. Here it is planted at the base of evergreen azaleas.

some will propagate from cuttings. Woody plants usually take a long time to reach transplant size from seed. Though many can be divided, it's generally easiest to propagate them from cuttings. Following are some tips on growing healthy shade plants and notes on each type of propagation.

Soil Improvement

After light intensity, nothing contributes more to the success of gardening in various shade conditions than having good soil. Generally speaking, shade-loving plants prefer a humus-rich soil with at least 8 inches (20cm) of well-decomposed organic material such as garden compost, leaf mold, or peat moss—and the deeper the soil, the better. Many shade-loving plants, such as garden lilies and daylilies, like good drainage, but a large number, such as Japanese primulas and flag iris, actually prefer a soil that is permanently moist and even boggy. Before planting a shade garden, always analyze the existing soil. If the soil looks hard and compacted or has tree roots close to the surface, do not attempt to cultivate the site. Any soil disturbance can kill the feeder roots of existing trees, since the feeder roots of most trees are in the first 12 inches (30cm) of topsoil. Instead, create a raised bed over the compacted soil by hauling in screened topsoil purchased from a local nursery.

Planting Among Exposed Tree Roots

Sometimes you will find trees that have thick tree roots exposed above the surface of the soil, forming "V" shaped pockets of soil. Small flowering plants can be inserted in these spaces to create a particularly beautiful shade planting, especially along a woodland path. Beech trees are a personal favorite because they have a natural tendency to expose their roots. At Cedaridge Farm we have a large ash tree with a beautiful network of roots, and we have planted among them clumps of perennial 'Barnhaven' primroses (below), checkered lily (a spring-flowering bulb), and biennial forget-me-nots. In another area we have masses of blue Siberian squill planted with yellow celandine for an early spring display.

Before planting between tree roots it is essential to dig down between the roots with a sharp, narrow, pointed trowel and to excavate as large and as deep a hole as possible. Discard the original compacted soil and replace with good topsoil, giving the roots of your flowering plants sufficient room in which to grow and thrive. If you run ino thick subsurface roots while excavating your planting hole between the exposed roots, do not cut through them, but work around the deeper roots, even using a table fork or an ice pick to scrape out the compacted soil.

To determine whether a site has good drainage, use a spade to dig a hole about 1 foot (30cm) wide and 2 feet (60cm) deep. Fill the hole with a bucket of water. If the water drains away within an hour, drainage is good. If the water still stands after several hours, then drainage is poor, and the site may be more suitable for bog plants.

To improve a poorly drained, shady site, you can make a raised bed using any number of materials, including bricks, stones, tree branches, and landscape ties. If you must include a tree in the raised bed area, keep the new soil away from its trunk by leaving a shallow depression between the soil and the bark. Soil piled high against a trunk can induce rot and kill a tree.

Soil can be classified as sand or clay in composition, with a happy medium called loam. A simple way of deciding what kind of soil your site has is to pick up a handful, squeeze it, and poke it with a finger. If the mass is made up of coarse granules and falls apart, it is sandy and has the disadvantage of offering poor moisture-holding capacity and poor anchorage. If the soil mass binds together and remains sticky after prodding, it is clayey and impervious. Clay soil not only puddles water on its surface, but also prevents roots from penetrating the soil in search of nutrients.

To improve compacted soil under trees, add plenty of peat moss, garden compost, or well-decomposed leaf mold, taking care not to damage any tree roots.

The best way to improve sandy or clay soil is to add humus. The least expensive form of humus combines garden compost, made from decomposed kitchen and garden waste, and leaf mold, made from decomposed shredded leaves. This homemade product takes time (usually 6 months) to decompose. Meanwhile, you may want to use some bales of peat from a garden center.

Because shade-loving plants like to grow in cool soil, it is important to use organic mulch materials not only for moisture retention but also as a weed barrier. Shredded leaves, wood chips, shredded pine bark, and pine needles make excellent natural mulches and are attractive in shady settings. In deeply shaded areas, however, you may want to use a white stone mulch like smooth beach pebbles or chunky landscape chips to increase light reflectiveness.

Another factor governing the performance of shade-loving plants is soil pH, a measure of the soil's acidity or alkalinity. Since most shade-loving plants are from wooded areas, they prefer an acid soil. Indeed, some plants like azaleas, hollies, and camellias require excessive amounts of acidity and timely applications of a high-acid fertilizer like Miracid or Hollytone. To test for soil pH, avoid store-bought soil test kits or pH meters, since they are unreliable and don't accurately explain how to correct an imbalance. Instead, obtain an analysis through a soil laboratory (local garden centers will provide the necessary information). This usually involves taking soil samples from various locations on your property, placing them in a pouch, and mailing them to a soil lab. You will receive a computer printout not only stating the soil pH but explaining how to correct any imbalances. If any nutrients are lacking in the soil, the printout will explain what they are and how to correct the deficiency. Acid soil

Above: Collecting a soil sample for a soil test is a simple task. Below: Leaves raked into a large bag are easily piled into an enclosure to decompose into precious leaf mold.

generally exists in places with woodland areas and high rainfall, while alkaline soil prevails in desert areas and where glaciers have scraped away topsoil down to subsurface limestone deposits. Alkaline soil often exists along house foundations where builders dump cement and aggregate waste, as well as in some agricultural soils where overfertilization has left salt deposits. Soil pH is measured on a scale from 1 to 14, with acid

The Magic of Leaf Mold

Perhaps no commodity is more precious for a successful shade garden than leaf mold, the product of decayed leaves. Made successfully, leaf mold is a fluffy, dark, sweet, yeasty-smelling, nutritious form of humus with ten times the water-holding capacity of unimproved topsoil. Leaf mold is almost impossible to buy from local nurseries because they generally use so much of it themselves. Make your own by building a bin of chicken wire to hold swept-up leaves gathered in autumn. Fine leaves like willow and pine needles can be raked onto a tarp and dragged to the wire enclosure, where they will decompose. However, large leaves like maple, oak, and hickory take such a long time to break down that they should be shredded first. To shred, either ride over the fallen leaves with a rider mower, or push a lawn mower over them before adding to the heap. Also, for speedy decomposition, it helps to add nitrogen (available from garden centers) to every 12-inch (30cm) layer of leaves and to turn the heap at monthly intervals. Nitrogen feeds the beneficial bacteria that aid in the decomposition process, while turning the heap introduces oxygen, which also helps the bacteria. Apply the leaves as a weed-suffocating mulch in spring and autumn. Even if the leaf mold is not completely broken down, add it at these times. Nature will finish the process, and your soil will become fluffy and fertile.

soil at the lower end of the scale. The remedy for acid soil is an application of lime and for alkaline soil the solution is an application of sulphur. But only a soil test can provide a good analysis and advice on amounts of soil conditioner to apply.

In areas where the soil is extremely hard or stony, you may want to dispense with any laborious attempt at subsurface soil improvement and create a level wooden deck on which to grow shade-loving plants in containers. Wooden decks can be extremely beautiful when built around existing trees, allowing the trunks to grow through the decks. The resulting canopy offers gently filtered light.

Lath Houses

When seedlings or cuttings of shade-loving plants are small, they need to be sized-up (grown to transplant size) outdoors in a nursery bed that is protected from drying out and from exposure to too much sun. At Cedaridge Farm, we have an old paddock area lightly shaded by spreading ash trees where we grow many transplants. Lacking a suitable shady site, the best alternative is a lath house—a structure made from wooden slats or black mesh (shade cloth)—supported overhead by posts. A lath house shades young plants until they are ready to be transferred to permanent locations.

In spring this lath house shelters delicate transplants. In summer it provides a good place to display shade-loving plants—such as these tuberous begonias—in hanging baskets.

Tunnel Houses

A tunnel house overwinters lots of young perennial plants, in this case hosta divisions, prior to transplanting to the garden in spring. The shade cloth prevents sunburned leaves.

Another structure to consider is a tunnel house, or cold house, which is a large-scale version of the traditional cold frame. While a cold frame is an unheated boxlike structure capable of holding a small number of plants through the winter, a cold house can accommodate thousands of plants. It is a long tunnellike structure with aluminum arches covered by clear plastic to provide protection from wind and freezing weather. To overwinter shade plants, the plastic is further covered with black netting to block the sun's rays. The unit can be unheated if hardy plants are to be propagated, because in addition to shading the primary need is for shelter.

Seed Starting

Seeds come in many different shapes and sizes, and have varying degrees of difficulty in germination. Many shade garden plants like coleus and impatiens have seeds that are extremely small and almost as fine as dust. They do not germinate well when seeded directly into the garden. Rather, they should be started indoors up to 10 weeks before outdoor planting, sown into a seed tray, and when large enough to handle (usually ¼ inch [6mm] high) transferred to individual pots to size-up. Greatest success is assured in a greenhouse or conservatory where seeds can receive bright filtered light and warm temperatures of at least 70°F (21°C). Lacking these conditions, consider using an artificial grow-light unit to start seeds. Plants that have reasonably large seeds often do well sown directly into the garden, provided that the soil is fluffy and clear of weeds. Hellebores and aconites, for example, set prodigious amounts of seed after flowering by forming plump pods that split open when the seeds are ripe. If seed is harvested fresh, it can be scattered about onto bare soil like chicken feed to establish new colonies. Although fresh seed from shade plants like primroses and hellebores may produce rapid germination, any delay in planting can induce a state of dormancy requiring winter chilling for germination. To accomplish this winter chilling, place seed packets in the vegetable bin of a refrigerator for a month or two before sowing.

Many shade-loving plants are susceptible to soilborne diseases such as damping-off, a fungus that attacks seedlings as they germinate, causing them to shrivel and die. This can be avoided by using only sterile pots and a sterile soil mix. Also, many shade plants are susceptible to drying out. Primrose seeds, for example, will die within an hour if the soil turns dry. To avoid rapid moisture loss after watering a seed tray, enclose it in a clear plastic bag (such as a kitchen freezer bag) until the seeds germinate. This creates a self-contained humid microclimate resistant to rapid dehydration.

Though ferns do not produce seeds, they can be propagated from tiny brown spores that usually form on the underside of leaves. Like specks of pepper, the spores will blow away if you breathe on them, but otherwise they can be treated like seeds. To propagate, pick a mature leaf that shows brown dot-size spore capsules, and shake the fern

frond over a piece of white paper. Then crease the paper to make a gutter and tap the spores onto a moist, peat-based potting soil in an open-necked glass jar. Cover the top with a sheet of clear plastic and store at room temperature in filtered bright light until tiny fern plants appear. When they are an inch (2.5cm) high, transfer them to individual pots to size-up before transplanting into their permanent positions in the garden.

Avoid using seeds from plant hybrids, since they may be sterile or unable to produce a quality plant in subsequent years.

Jack-in-the-pulpit seeds are enclosed in red berries. Easy to handle, the seeds germinate readily in acid soil. (Use caution if you have young children, because both the berries and the seeds are poisonous.)

How to Establish Self-Seeding Colonies

There are many shade-loving plants that will self-seed and establish self-perpetuating colonies. At Cedaridge Farm we now have large self-seeding colonies of cardinal flowers, hellebores, dwarf crested iris, forget-me-nots, winter aconites, English primroses (below), Japanese primroses, and checkered lilies. The trick is to ensure that when the seed pods ripen the seeds can scatter and fall onto bare, fluffy soil. Soil that is compacted or covered in weed growth inhibits germination. With hellebores and aconites I look to see when the seed pods start to swell and split open, revealing dark brown or black seeds. Then I shake the seeds into a brown bag, and scatter them where I want new colonies to grow.

I have found that the best way to ensure self-seeding of Japanese primroses is to cluster groups of stones among the original colony. Japanese primroses thrive in boggy soil, and sometimes during heavy rains the area will flood and wash the seeds in a particular direction. As the wash strikes the stones, the seeds are trapped, and they readily germinate among the stones. Without the stones to hold the tiny seeds they can be flushed away.

I am always alert to self-sown plants because they are a good indication that a larger colony can be established. I then plant the area more thickly to increase the chance of self-seeding.

Bulb Division

You can harvest lily bulbils from the leaf axils of flowering stems to propagate new plants.

Most flowering bulbs like daffodils and gladiolus produce bulblets around the mother bulb. After the leaves die down the plant can be dug up and the smaller bulbs separated for transplanting to a nursery bed. Daffodils will size-up without any protection. Gladiolus, however, is tender to freezing and needs a covering of thick mulch during winter to help the bulblets survive. On the other hand, you can store tender bulblets indoors during freezing weather and transplant them after frost danger in spring to size-up. Some lilies produce not only bulblets around the mother bulb but also bulbils in the leaf axils along the stem. Pea-size and black, they can be treated like seeds, sown into a seed tray to sprout and size-up before transplanting. Each bulbil will produce an exact replica of the parent.

Root Division

The vast majority of hardy perennials, such as hostas and ferns, can be propagated by root division, usually done in spring or late summer in the third year of maturity. Simply take a spade or garden fork and dig around the established clump. Wash away soil from the roots with a jet of water and you will see how the root mass is composed of sections or divisions, which can be pried apart. Usually you end up with small and large divisions, each with a crown of leaves or immature buds. The large divisions can be transplanted directly into the garden, but the small divisions are best potted and placed in your tunnel house or under your lath house to size-up.

These flag iris divisions were taken from three-year-old clumps. Clip the tops of the leaves when you transplant, or the plants will keel over in wind, uprooting themselves.

Cuttings

Most woody plants, including camellias, azaleas, and rhododendrons, are propagated from tip cuttings. Others, like ivy, yellow archangel, and vinca, can be propagated from stem cuttings, meaning that any section of stem with a leaf node can be rooted to form a new plant. A third type of cutting, known as a root cutting, can yield enormous numbers of new plants because every section of underground root, when cut into 2-inch (5cm) segments, is capable of sprouting new roots and a crown of leaves.

To take a tip cutting, use a sharp hand pruner to cut a 6-inch (15cm) section of stem. Strip away the lower leaves, and scrape the bark for 2 inches (5cm) at the bottom of the stem with a knife. Then insert the tip end up to half its length in a pot filled with a moist, peat-based potting soil. Groups of cuttings can be started in a single pot, provided they do not touch and there is air circulation among them. Enclose the cuttings and pot in a clear plastic bag, gathering the neck over the cuttings with a twist-tie so that the bag creates a humid microclimate. Place the pot in bright filtered light.

When taking pachysandra cuttings, you need only strip away lower leaves to expose the stem and put stems in a container of tepid water. Change the water at weekly intervals until a root system develops along the stems (usually 8 weeks), then transplant.

Examine the cuttings at twice-weekly intervals, and after rooting has taken place, transfer them to individual pots to increase in size. The success rate of cuttings is greatly increased if the cut end is first dusted with rooting hormone, a white powdery substance available from garden centers.

To take stem cuttings, cut long sections of stem into segments, ensuring that each segment has a leaf node from which new roots can sprout. The leaves above the node can

These anemone seedlings have reached transplant size. The seeds are first started in a seed-starting tray, then separated individually into the pots until they are ready to be set out into the garden.

be left in place, but the leaves below the node should be removed. Insert the naked bottom portion into the soil so that the node is covered. A group of stem cuttings can be planted together in a pot or propagating tray and enclosed in clear plastic to encourage rooting.

Some plants are so easy to propagate from tip or stem cuttings that they need only water in which to root. Examples are English ivy, pachysandra, coleus, and impatiens.

Bleeding heart is an example of a shade-loving plant with a root system able to sprout new plants from sections of root. After the leaves die in summer, lift the entire plant and cut some of the roots into 2- to 3-inch (5 to 7.5cm) sections. Place the cuttings horizontally onto a pot or propagating tray, and cover with ½ inch (12mm) of soil. The parent plant can then be replanted and root cuttings placed in bright, filtered shade to sprout roots and grow new plants.

Designing Shade Gardens

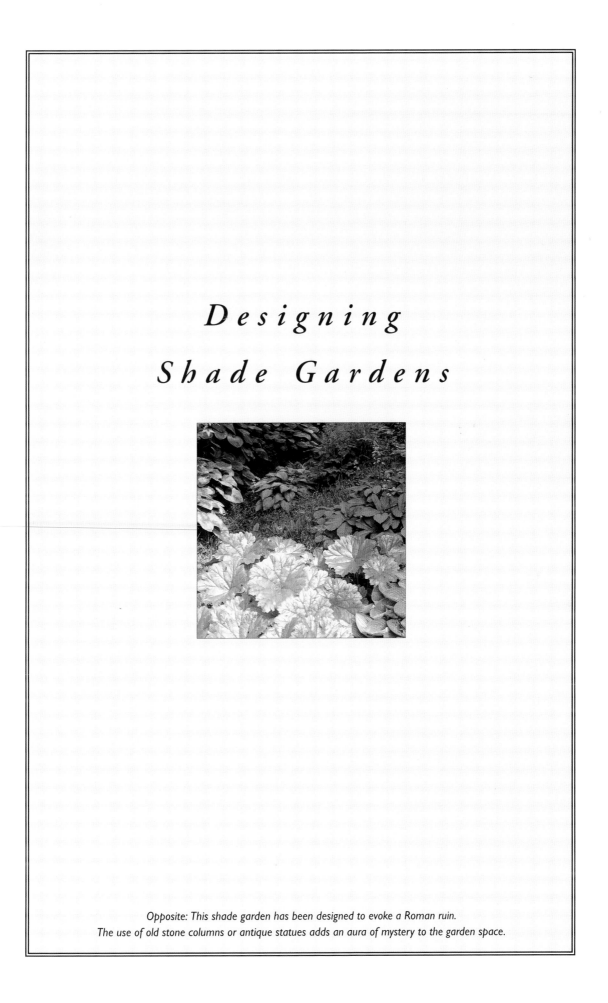

Opposite: This shade garden has been designed to evoke a Roman ruin.
The use of old stone columns or antique statues adds an aura of mystery to the garden space.

Every garden design project must start with a few basic decisions. After assessing the site for light intensity and soil composition, you must decide whether to do the project yourself or hire a contractor, and whether the design will be formal or informal. You must also resolve whether to provide maximum interest at a particular time of year (spring is when most shade-loving plants bloom) or plan for year-round interest, and whether the emphasis should be on softscape (plants) or hardscape (wood and stone) materials.

Generally, a formal design is more expensive and requires help from a garden designer and a contractor, while informal designs are much easier to implement without professional help. Also, formality in a shade garden invariably involves costly paving, walls, flights of steps, balustrades, and terraces to establish the formal lines, while informal designs generally place a greater emphasis on plants and natural elements such as gravel or wood chip paths. Formal designs work especially well in city locations. For example, the southern cities of Savannah, Georgia, and Charleston, South Carolina, are world-famous for their formal courtyard gardens that function as outdoor garden rooms. Informal gardens work well where shade comes mostly from trees, since disrupting the soil can be lethal to established woody plants. These, however, are general

Contrasts of sunlight and shadow, hardscape and softscape are beguiling elements of this Japanese-style garden.

Design Ideas for Shady Spaces

• On level sites, consider building your design around a shady lawn or a series of shady lawns connected by grassy paths. Fescues are shade-tolerant grasses for light- to medium-shaded situations.

• On sloping sites, consider a series of rock shelves or rock terraces and a stream with waterfalls fed by recirculating water, since the combination of stone, trees, and water is natural and very appealing.

• Design for shadow effects. Especially attractive are the long shadows drawn across the lawn by the rising or setting sun. Create dappled shadow patterns along paths by inserting breaks in the leaf canopy.

• Seek pronounced vertical lines from trees and shrubs. If a tall tree like wild cherry or a billowing rhododendron shrub has a thicket of low branches obscuring the view, thin them out. Accentuate instead the plant's pleasing upward silhouette, and open the leaf canopy to show blue sky, a sunlit lawn, or a water feature. To hide the mundane tree trunks of ashes and poplars, plant decorative evergreen vines like needlepoint ivy and silver euonymus. Seek out trees and shrubs with decorative bark. White birch, honey birch, paperbark maple, and red-twig dogwood will add texture and color to many shade gardens.

• Visualize your landscape as a canvas and divide it into three distinct zones: the overhead tree canopy, the understory, and the ground level. Try to emphasize these three levels of interest by using ground-hugging plants like hostas, forget-me-nots, and ferns for the base; small trees and shrubs like azaleas, dogwoods, and camellias for eye-level interest; and towering shade trees like tulip poplars, honey locusts, and beeches for soaring, sky-high beauty. I like to think of my shade garden as a cathedral, with tree branches representing vaulting columns, understory plants as stained glass windows and tapestries, and groundcovers in place of rich carpeting.

• For the most part, a design that relies more on foliage, texture, and structural interest is easier to maintain than a design that depends on flowering plants.

If you have no mature shade trees or hardscape elements that cast strong shadows, you can create some shade with an arbor or pergola covered with fast-growing vines. Planted at the base of this arbor is a collection of astilbes and heartleaf, while the cross-beams hold hanging baskets.

guidelines, since an informal garden can look sensational on a city plot and a formal garden can be a wonderful surprise in natural woodland!

The amount of softscape and hardscape depends on the type of design desired and the amount of time you are able to devote to caring for plants, since plants are perishable and need more attention than durable hardscape elements. At my home, Cedaridge Farm, we decided on mostly informal garden spaces because they are more in harmony with the atmosphere of our two-hundred-year-old farmhouse. At first, we gave little thought to structures, concentrating our efforts on establishing a circuitous path around the property and on providing color through large plantings of daffodils, azaleas, peonies, hellebores, and primroses. Once these broad sweeps of color were in place, we added structures at strategic intervals—bridges along the path to crisscross a stream, a gazebo to provide a focal point at the end of a vista, benches to provide places for pausing and enjoying a view, and rustic arches to act as transitional elements along the way.

Popular Shade Garden Designs

There are many types of shade gardens to consider, depending on the source of your shade, the size of your garden, and the topography of the land. Shade gardens range in scope from large woodland gardens to small shaded water gardens that can fit into the corner of a courtyard. In my garden, I have them all. Some of my shade gardens are no more than island beds encircling trees and filled with an assortment of flowering plants, while others depend on foliage interest to cut down maintenance. A meandering path connects them all, so visitors can enjoy a visual adventure, with some spaces designed for privacy and introspection and others for breathtaking vistas.

Wildlife Gardens

The presence of desirable wildlife like songbirds and butterflies can enhance your enjoyment of a garden. The four essentials for attracting wildlife are the presence of water in the form of a pool, pond, or stream; food plants like berry bushes; cover such as evergreen trees and twiggy deciduous shrubs to provide security; and nest and butterfly boxes. Overhead cover is especially important because songbirds like a leafy canopy to discourage hawk attacks.

The staff at your local wildlife center can help you decide which local indigenous plants to use but the following

Tulip poplar trees, with their tall slender trunks and tracery of arching branches, create a "cathedral" effect above an understory of azaleas. English ivy decorates a tree trunk along the path.

ideas will guide you in providing for wildlife. For food plants, consider blueberries, bayberries, viburnum, holly, and crabapple. Water can be added as a free-form pool with a flexible liner, a small pool using a rigid plastic liner,

A grove of flowering dogwoods underplanted with daffodils presents a glittering spectacle in spring.

or a pedestal-mounted birdbath. A submersible heater installed in a birdbath provides a lasting supply of warm water, a critical winter need for birds.

Evergreen trees and shrubs, including juniper, hemlock, pines, and holly, will provide year-round protective cover. Intersperse deciduous shrubs among these, notably red-twig dogwood, barberry, winterberry (which attracts bluebirds), or multiflora rose (which attracts cardinals).

Rock, log, and mulch piles also offer effective cover. Birds especially like to rummage about in compost in search of centipedes and worms, while many amphibians, reptiles, and small mammals will use them as hiding places.

Along the paths install nest boxes for wrens and chickadees. These have small holes and lack perches so that blue jays cannot stand on them to extend a leg inside and grab eggs or young.

A Woodland Garden

A winding wood-chip path and a teak English-style garden bench are focal points in this design, with drifts of shade-loving plants lining the woodland walk. Structural interest is provided by redbuds and birch trees pruned of their lower branches to emphasize their sinuous trunk silhouettes. Ivy is allowed to climb the more mature trees, offering a lush decorative effect.

A Foxgloves *(Digitalis purpurea)*

B 'Barnhaven' primroses *(Primula × polyantha* 'Barnhaven')

C Maidenhair ferns *(Adiantum pedatum)*

D Bleeding-hearts *(Dicentra spectabilis)*

E Spanish bluebells *(Hyacinthoides hispanica,* also called *Endymion hispanicus* and *Scilla hispanica)*

F Wild columbine, mixed colors *(Aquilegia canadensis)*

G Lenten rose *(Helleborus orientalis)*

H Hakone grass *(Hakonechloa macra)*

I 'Penny' viola, mixed colors *(Viola* 'Penny')

J Heartleaf bergenia *(Bergenia cordifolia)*

K Asiatic lily *(Lilium* 'Asiatic' hybrids)

L False spirea, mixed colors *(Astilbe × arendsii)*

M 'Viette' goldenstar *(Chrysogonum virginianum* 'Viette')

N Dame's rocket, mixed colors *(Hesperis matronalis)*

O Leopard's bane *(Doronicum caudatum)*

P Ostrich fern *(Matteuccia struthiopteris)*

Q Rhododendron *(Rhododendron* spp.)

R Lilies, Oriental hybrids *(Lilium* hybrids)

S Cardinal flower *(Lobelia cardinalis)*

T 'Luxuriant' bleeding heart *(Dicentra* 'Luxuriant')

U Forget-me-not *(Myosotis alpestris)*

V Snakeroot *(Cimicifuga* spp.)

W Azalea, mixed colors *(Rhododendron* spp.)

X Redbud tree *(Cercis canadensis)*

Y 'Heritage' river birch *(Betula nigra* 'Heritage')

Z English ivy *(Hedera helix)*

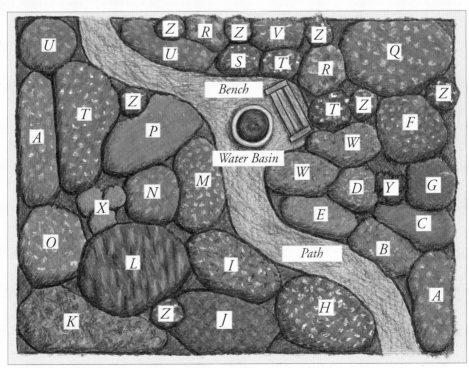

Woodland Gardens

The making of a romantic woodland garden depends on whether woodland exists on the site or whether you must create a wooded lot using fast-growing trees. Existing woodland will most likely be an impenetrable wilderness, choked with brambles and filled with dead or dying trees and dense thickets of thorny shrubs like multiflora rose.

In this case, the first priority is to penetrate the tangle. Note any desirable indigenous elements like ponds, streams, or rocky outcrops. Then consider where to make

Carpeting Effects

By choosing certain tall flowering shrubs and trees, it's possible to color the ground with a natural confetti created from spent blossoms or colorful leaves. Some plants retain their blossoms or leaves for a long time. By the time their petals or leaves are ready to drop, they have withered to an earth brown color. But there is an elite group of plants that will drop their petals or leaves for a magnificent carpeting effect. Here are some of the best hardy kinds:

Acer palmatum (Japanese maple)—red and orange leaves

Acer rubrum (red maple)—red or orange leaves

Cercis canadensis (redbud)—rose pink petals

Ginkgo biloba (ginkgo)—yellow leaves

Laburnum vossi (laburnum)—yellow petals

Magnolia soulangiana (saucer magnolia)—white and pink petals

Malus species (crabapple)—red, pink, and white petals

Philadelphus coronarius (mock orange)—white petals

Prunus triloba (flowering cherry)—pink petals

Rhododendron hybrids (rhododendron)—red, pink, and white petals

Styrax japonicus (silverbell)—white petals

Wisteria floribunda (wisteria)—blue petals

A rich carpeting effect is created with the fallen leaves of Japanese maple. Once the leaves turn brown they are raked up and composted.

paths that take advantage of existing contours in the terrain. Using a machete to clear a passage, tie ribbons to branches to show where a path can lead, and start clearing along the route. You will probably need several other tools to accomplish this, including a spade, ax, or pickax for grubbing up obstinate roots. A hand pruner is useful for cutting through small branches, while with a long-handled pruner you can tackle larger branches. You may also need a hand saw and a chain saw to clear away unwanted trees like black walnuts, which have roots that poison soil, or sumac, which can be highly invasive. If all this sounds daunting, hire someone to clear the site.

To inscribe a path, take a rake and scratch the soil, removing all weedy growth and leaf litter. Then lay down a mulch that will deter further weed growth and also feel comfortable to walk on. Some excellent mulches to consider are pine needles, shredded pine bark, and gravel. Evaluate the direction of the path, allowing it to make natural curves and turns. For maximum use of the space, avoid straight lines and encourage hairpin bends that allow the path to turn back onto itself, especially where there are descending slopes. It's a good idea to define the edges of your path with heavy tree branches or boulders, especially in places where the mulch can be washed away. On steep sections, use steps made from thick tree branches or old railroad ties. Mark places along the path where you can establish colonies of flowers, especially native woodland wildflowers and ferns.

Although mixed perennial borders look good edging sunny lawns, in woodland they tend to look unnatural. It is far better to plant in broad brush strokes of color, allowing plants to form drifts that merge into each other.

Lucky is the gardener who uncovers large boulders, for these make wonderful accents along paths. If boulders are absent, haul some from a local quarry and place them at the bend in a path, or build low, rough fieldstone walls to meander along sections of

Not all trees display green leaves in summer. Many have bronze or silver foliage, while the Norway maples shown here offer cream and yellow leaves.

the path. Consider yourself fortunate if you uncover a small stream or pond, because these features also make charming accents when decorated with plants that can spill into the water.

If you must create your woodland from nothing, seek advice from local tree nurseries about fast-growing trees for your area. Several that are widely adapted include the river birch *(Betula nigra),* especially the 'Heritage' strain; dawn redwood *(Metasequoia glyptostroboides);* and tulip poplars *(Liriodendron tulipifera).* You can start with small plants, since they can grow 5 feet (1.5m) per year. Woodland that you create from scratch does not need to be a diverse mixture of trees. Indeed, using one type of tree to make a grove can look sensational. Trees with decorative bark, such as white birch for the Northeast and redwoods for coastal California and the Pacific Northwest, work particularly well in groves.

Shady Water Gardens

What is more romantic or uplifting in all of nature than a series of sparkling waterfalls cascading down a shady slope, splashing musically from one pool to another, with cushions of moss and feathery ferns making a haven of tranquillity? Ponder a mysterious, mirror-smooth pool with a white water lily gleaming from its center and bleeding hearts, azaleas, and hostas along the rim. Imagine the drama of sunlight striking the water through gaps in the overhead leaf canopy or morning mist lingering over the pond.

Where water features do not already exist, you can introduce them using either rigid preformed liners for small pools or flexible liners for larger ones. A submerged pump recirculates the water and a filter keeps it clean. Although you can make watertight pools from concrete and packed clay, flexible or rigid liners are more efficient and economical, their bases hidden by the reflective quality of the water and their rims covered with stones.

To make a recirculating stream, you must bury a pipe along the stream's length to return water from the bottom of the pool to the top. The placement of boulders and rocks

This shady rock garden at Cedaridge Farm features a tiny cascade and water lily pool. 'Bowles Golden' grass, planted beside the nymph, displays its best color in shade.

to create waterfalls and pools is important, for they must not only look as though they have been sitting there for years, but they must be sited to avoid erosion to stream banks during periods of excessive rain and flooding. In some cases, rocks are best seated in concrete covered with a spreading groundcover like vinca. Creating deep soil pockets among the boulders is useful for growing desirable plants.

Four kinds of plants are suitable for shady water gardens: water plants like water lilies and Japanese iris, which thrive with their roots permanently submerged in water; bog plants like Japanese primroses, which like to be in permanently moist or muddy soil; marginal plants, such as astilbe and lady's mantle, which tolerate alternate flooding and drying provided they are planted in a humus-rich soil; and oxygenators, which are vital to fish and amphibians. Oxygenators generally live beneath the water or float on the surface and help to maintain a healthy, oxygen-rich environment to sustain aquatic creatures. Examples of oxygenators are cabomba (*Cabomba caroliniana*) and anacharis (*Elodea canadensis*), both fernlike plants that make good breeding habitats for fish.

Surprisingly, hardy white water lilies can tolerate light shade, provided they receive some direct sunlight for 3 to 5 hours. Some cultivars are more shade-tolerant than others—'Chromatella' (yellow), 'Attraction' (pink), and

A dramatic Italian-style shade garden at Blake House (owned by the University of California at Berkeley) features a highly formal layout that includes a rectangular water lily pool.

'Comanche' (orange), for example, are fine water lilies for partially shaded spots. For small pools, water plants grow best in containers, since this allows them to be fertilized easily for maximum bloom production and keeps more aggressive plants like lotus and water lilies within bounds.

Goldfish and koi are ideal for stocking small streams and pools. They are not only beautiful but also are easy to care for and readily become tame, taking food from your fingers.

Arched Passageways

Of the possible features in a shade garden, one of the most appealing is a leafy tunnel made from the arched branches of tall trees and shrubs meeting overhead or from vine-covered pergolas and passageways. Garden centers sell metal-rod arches for constructing arched passageways. Monet-style arches—inspired by the Grande Allée, a rose-covered tunnel in the Impressionist painter's garden at Giverny—are among the loveliest you

In woodland gardens it is important to provide strong structural elements, such as the sinuous trunks of these rhododendrons, pruned of their lower branches to frame the misty clearing.

can buy. Spacious proportions, 7 feet (2.1m) high and 5 feet (1.5m) wide, make this type of arch suitable for a shady entrance or as a transitional feature along a garden walkway. The 10-foot (3m)-long Monet-style pergola can create a shady tunnel that connects two garden spaces or can lead the gaze to a garden feature, such as a fountain or sculpture.

At Cedaridge Farm, we strategically place rustic arches along paths leading from one shade garden to another. Made from cedar posts cut from our own woodland, we find them more attractive than metal arches. We also have a leaf tunnel, which we first recognized as an appealing shade garden feature during a visit to Cézanne's garden at Aix-en-Provence in southern France. Cézanne, another Impressionist painter, liked to paint the countryside around his family's home, which was framed by the arching branches of sycamore and chestnut trees. When he bought a property with an acre (4,047 sq m) of sloping ground, he promptly planted fast-growing redbud trees, golden chain trees, and mock orange shrubs along rustic paths so that they formed leaf tunnels.

Using trees that bloom and flowering shrubs for leaf tunnels is especially effective because when the flowers fade they will drop their petals on the path, coloring it briefly as if with confetti.

Tapestry Gardens

Tapestry gardens, also known as foliage gardens, contain plants chosen for the contrasting colors, textures, and shapes of their leaves. Boring? Not in the least, provided you choose foliage of varying size, iridescence, and translucence, particularly among plants with variegated leaves.

Tapestry gardens are most often seen in tropical climates, where exotic leaf forms such as those of bananas, palms, cactuses, and bromeliads can be used. Yet the most impressive tapestry garden I ever encountered was at Bois de Moutiers, Varengeville, on the Normandy coast. The garden designer,

A narrow, grassy path cuts through a tapestry of foliage contrasts. The flowering rhododendrons are merely icing on the cake.

Guillaume Mallet, took swatches of fabrics and tried to match their colors and textures with trees and shrubs. He used blue Atlas cedars for blue chenille, ostrich ferns for green lace, gunnera to imitate dark green velvet, massed red rhododendrons for red silk, and the blistered leaves of hostas for brocade. The tapestry garden at Bois de Moutiers occupies an entire coastal ravine, but small-scale tapestry gardens can easily achieve a similar effect with compact, low-growing perennials and woody plants.

A favorite foliage planting at Cedaridge Farm combines the heart-shaped leaves of sweet violets, the delicate lacelike leaves of maidenhair ferns, and the paddle-shaped leaves of blue hostas with shimmering highlights from variegated euonymus, silver-leaf caladiums, 'Glacier' English ivy, and 'Bowles Golden' grass.

Moss Gardens

I've never seen anything more spiritually uplifting than the serene moss gardens of Kyoto, Japan, where cushions of velvety green moss soothe the senses. On entering these tranquil religious domains, I always feel the urge to lie down and fall peacefully asleep. Be aware, however, that a moss garden is probably the most labor-intensive theme garden you could ever hope to plant. It is highly sensitive to drought and heavy foot traffic, in need of constant watering during summer dry spells, and creating the ideal medium for the germination of weed seeds, so weeding is a constant chore. The installation of a sprinkler system to keep moss lush and green through summer considerably reduces maintenance chores.

This Japanese-style moss garden, set in a Pennsylvania woodland, is modeled after the monastery gardens of Kyoto. To achieve this degree of lushness the moss needs constant watering, diligent weeding, and acid soil.

Blue for Shady Areas

The French Impressionist painter Claude Monet liked to paint shadowy areas blue because he recognized that shade is often imbued with blue tones, especially in the cool light of early morning. In his garden he loved to plant shady areas with blue flowers to heighten the blue tones. One of Monet's favorite flowers for achieving this effect was the forget-me-not (below), but there are other good blue plants for shade, including bluebells, browallia, bugleweed, blue creeping phlox, blue geraniums, blue hostas, blue hydrangeas, dwarf blue irises, Jacob's ladder, lilyturf, blue pansies, Siberian bugloss, blue violets, Virginia bluebells, periwinkle, and wishbone flowers. Consider making blue the predominant color in your shade garden, adding other colors as complements. For example, Monet liked to plant blue with pink for a beautiful color harmony, and also frequently combined blue with yellow.

On the upside, moss tolerates even deep shade, and you don't need much to make a good impression. A mossy bank beside a bend in a woodland path, a mossy edging to a shady section of stream, or a carpet of moss encircling a boulder or stone ornament can add a note of distinction.

If patches of moss already exist on your land, then you probably have a suitable environment for it, because moss readily spreads in damp, humus-rich soils. The trick is having it take hold precisely where you want it and making it lush, luxuriant, and devoid of bare spots. Start by hauling screened topsoil, well-decomposed compost, or decayed leaf mold to build hummocks on which to grow the moss. Ensure an acid soil by adding sulphur. Then dig up clumps of moss and lay them together like sections of turf grass over the prepared bed. An alternate method, especially if you have a small amount of moss, is to crumble the moss over a soil bed or rock ledge so that tiny spores hidden among the leaves are released. Then water regularly. Covering rocks or soil with buttermilk helps moss take hold quickly, since buttermilk creates a culture in which spores can germinate. Good companions for moss are ferns and hostas.

Fern Gardens

Ferns range in size from small "button" ferns that can grow among tiny cracks in walls to tall, towering tree ferns that look like palm trees. While some have traditional fern leaves with soft, arching, feathery fronds, the leaf shapes also include the straplike foliage of hart's tongue fern and the leathery, indented leaves of staghorns. More than ten thousand species range worldwide from the sub-Arctic to the sub-Antarctic. None produce flowers, though some, like the cinnamon fern, produce interesting brown spore-bearing stems that resemble flower spikes.

Though ferns are most often used as background plants in shade gardens, it is possible to create a beautiful garden space using them exclusively. Collections of ferns look most attractive in natural settings, particularly near water features and boulders. Northern gardeners cannot grow tender tree ferns and staghorns unless the plants are confined to containers that can be moved indoors during freezing winter weather.

The Morris Arboretum in Philadelphia has perhaps the most ingenious small-space fern garden ever designed. It is a sunken garden set in a grove of trees to provide shade. A flight of stone steps leads down to a path that encircles a pool on the inside and is bordered by rocky ledges on the outside. Ferns are planted in pockets among the rocks so that they cascade from overhead. At the far end of the pool, a wooden bridge overhung with Australian tree ferns crosses a spillway where water cascades into a grotto, the edges of which drip with maidenhair ferns. Beyond the bridge, the path steps down through a stone arch and up the other side to a flight of steep steps leading to an observation platform on top of the arch.

Cushiony soft, star-shaped whorls of haircap moss contrast well with variegated euonymus and a cluster of boulders. Haircap moss is one of the most drought-tolerant and shade-tolerant mosses.

Though the fern garden at the Morris Arboretum is in a heated Victorian-style conservatory to accommodate some tender tropical species, a similar planting could be accomplished using hardy ferns that can survive northern winters. Other suitable structural elements for fern gardens include fallen logs and tree stumps with ferns planted in the hollows or a deer statue standing in a colony of low-growing hay-scented and sensitive ferns. Most hardy ferns are deciduous, their fronds turning brown and dying down in winter, then sprouting again in spring as fiddle-heads. Some, like the Christmas fern (*Polystichum acrostichoides*), are evergreen.

The Fern Garden at the Morris Arboretum features tender species such as Australian tree ferns, and so must be housed in a protective conservatory.

Japanese Shade Garden Ideas

Traditional Japanese gardens provide lots of inspiration for shade garden designs. If you cannot visit Kyoto, Japan, with its fine imperial gardens that date back three hundred years, then you may be able to tour the Portland Japanese Garden (Oregon), the Seattle Japanese Garden, Swiss Pines Japanese Garden (Philadelphia), or the Japanese Garden at the Missouri Botanical Garden (St. Louis).

The Japanese are masters at pruning. Many of their shade garden shrubs and trees are pruned of all lower branches. This pruning leaves slender multiple trunks that radiate upward, making it possible to look between them to a clearing beyond. Foliage contrasts are also evident, especially in the willowlike leaves of bamboo, the fleecelike foliage of cut-leaf Japanese maple, and the glossy, jadelike, spear-shaped leaves of camellias. Three-quarters of the trees tend to be evergreen—both needle evergreens (like junipers and pines) and broadleaf evergreens (like azaleas and camellias). These plants are often sheared to create the impression of a landscape of rolling hills.

Color is introduced with subtle seasonal accents—pink cherry blossoms in spring, blue Japanese irises in summer, and the silky plumes of ornamental grasses in autumn. Pools fed by streams introduce the important element of water, while hillsides are scoured for interesting boulders to introduce strong structural accents and for stepping-stones to lay across hummocks of moss. This combination of elements, together with strategically placed stone towers and stone lanterns, looks especially beautiful in winter after a light covering of snow.

Hosta Gardens

Native mostly to Japan, hostas are not as large a family as ferns, but the forty wild species have been hybridized to create as broad a selection as ferns. Hostas are the most popular of all perennial plants for shade, not only for their handsome paddle-shaped leaves but also for their conspicuous flower spikes, which can be as tall as foxgloves and as pleasantly fragrant as gardenias. For the best effect, plant hostas primarily for their leaf colors and enjoy the blue, purple, or white flowers as a bonus.

This ribbon of hostas includes a mixture of varieties. In early spring the space is alive with a dense planting of daffodils; the withering daffodil leaves of late spring are conveniently covered by the emerging hosta leaves.

Most hostas are low, spreading plants with leaves that arch out to create a weed-suffocating groundcover. When massed in a theme garden of their own, they should be planted to create a patchwork quilt effect of contrasting leaf colors. Since they are hardy deciduous plants, the leaves of many varieties turn golden yellow in autumn and sprout new growth in early spring as soon as a warming trend sets in.

At Cedaridge Farm, our hosta garden places a heavy emphasis on five outstanding varieties: *Hosta sieboldiana* 'Elegans' for its huge, blue, blistered leaves; *Hosta undulata* 'Medio-picta' for its bright white and green variegation; *Hosta* 'Gold Standard' for its golden-yellow leaves edged with blue-green; *Hosta* 'Royal Standard', which displays lustrous chartreuse leaves; and *Hosta* 'Frances Williams', a blue and cream sport of *Hosta sieboldiana*.

Given deep, humus-rich, fertile soil and good drainage, some of the larger hybrids like 'Sum and Substance' and 'Blue Angel' will grow as tall as a person and create a corridor of big, beautiful leaves when planted on either side of a path.

All-Season Shade Garden

Planted in a circle around a few trees, this charming garden may be small but it has a big impact. Most of the plants in the design are continuous-flowering varieties (such as begonias and impatiens) or colorful foliage types (such as caladiums and hostas), which provide color throughout the growing season. The beautiful bark of the 'Heritage' river birch ensures ornamental interest even in winter.

A   'Heritage' river birch (*Betula nigra* 'Heritage')

B   'Starbright' impatiens (*Impatiens* 'Starbright')

C   'Wizard' coleus, mixed colors (*Coleus* 'Wizard')

D   'Luxuriant' bleeding heart (*Dicentra* 'Luxuriant')

E   Rainbow plant, mix of cultivars (*Caladium* × *hortulanum*)

F   Ostrich fern (*Matteuccia struthiopteris*)

G   'Non-Stop' begonias, mixed colors (*Begonia tuberhybrida* 'Non-Stop')

H   'Blue Angel' and 'Sum and Substance' hostas (*Hosta* 'Blue Angel' and *H.* 'Sum and Substance')

I   'Viette' goldenstar (*Chrysogonum virginianum* 'Viette')

J   'Blue Bells' browallia (*Browallia* 'Blue Bells')

An Island Bed around a Tree

A single tree is a perfect place to plant an island bed, which can be circular or kidney-shaped for a natural look. For a more formal look, the bed can be square or rectangular, but this is usually in conflict with the billowing circular leaf canopy. Though these island beds can be simple mounds of soil around a tree into which plants are set, it is better to use an edging of heavy tree branches or stones to keep the raised soil in place. This is vital if the tree is situated on a slope.

Plantings around Ornamental Bark

One of my favorite shade plantings combines the ornamental qualities of tree bark with flowering plants or decorative foliage, for example, hellebores planted around the base of a paperbark maple (*Acer griseum*) or winter aconites surrounding a red-twig dogwood (*Cornus sericea*). The favored tree for decorative bark is the white birch (also known as silver birch, paper birch, and New England birch), but at Cedaridge Farm we have difficulty keeping white birches alive because of summer heat stress and borer infestations.

A very good alternative to white birches has proven to be the 'Heritage' strain of river birch (*Betula nigra*), with its beautiful honey-colored, peeling bark. Other good trees and shrubs with ornamental bark include moosewood (*Acer pennsylvanica*), quaking aspen (*Populus tremuloides*), Japanese stewartia (*Stewartia pseudocamellia*), and the yellow-twig dogwood (*Cornus sericea* 'Flaviramea'). Note that on both the red-twig and yellow-twig dogwood, the best coloration is on new growth and therefore it is best to prune plants back to the base every year, in the late spring, so they are forced to sprout new brightly colored juvenile shoots for decorative winter effect.

Sometimes, in order to fully expose the decorative quality of bark, it is necessary to prune away lower branches. If the tree or shrub has multiple trunks, it may be best to selectively thin out some of the trunks so that the colorful lines of just a few are accentuated.

Island beds are especially desirable around trees with compacted soil or under trees with a dense canopy where grass cannot grow. Soil is generally hard and compacted from the trunk of a tree to its drip line, since this area is invariably crisscrossed with feeder roots. Even if the soil can be fluffed up, the tree's feeder roots are likely to rob the new plantings of soil and nutrients. It's therefore best to ensure a raised planting area of at least 8 to 12 inches (20 to 30cm). Avoid soil contact with the trunk, however, because covering too much trunk with soil can induce rot.

Plant island beds with one variety such as 'Nonstop' begonias or with a mixture of annuals, perennials, and bulbs for flowers and foliage.

Naturalizing

This term describes a style of planting that tries to imitate nature by establishing a self-perpetuating colony. When you walk through an English woodland, home to vast expanses of primroses and bluebells, or enter an Appalachian glen spangled with blue creeping phlox and white foamflowers, you will see these wildflowers in generous drifts or sweeps of color, happily multiplying by self-seeding or by sending out underground roots called stolons.

Some wildflowers (lady slipper orchids, for example) can be difficult to naturalize because they demand such a particular climatic or soil condition that you'll be lucky to grow just a clump or two. Other plant species are easy to naturalize, especially perennials like hellebores and bulbs like daffodils.

For successful naturalizing, keep your site weed-free. Even plants such as early-flowering snowdrops that bloom when there is no competition from weeds will dwindle if annual or perennial weeds invade the site later in the season. To keep weed populations down, stockpile fallen leaves and shred them with a lawn mower to make them

This naturalized planting features blue Quaker ladies, a North American wildflower, with native azaleas growing in the background.

light, fluffy, and easy to handle. Then use the shredded leaves as a mulch to keep down weeds. If any aggressive weeds do penetrate the mulch barrier, it is easy to selectively remove them by hand.

On slopes where indigenous soil can be thin and rocky, consider creating some terraces to hold back strips of new soil. These don't have to be elaborate, just lines of tree branches or stones that can make level, stepped areas.

This shade planting at Cedaridge Farm features azaleas in drifts of one color and a native redbud tree in a similar color. Underplanted daffodils will naturalize as the years go by.

Designing for Lawn Shadows

The beginning and the end of the day are usually the best times to visit a shade garden. When the sun is poised low in the sky, it pencils the landscape with strong shadow contrasts. These long shadows can look sensational when they streak across sections of green lawn. Morning light is usually cool, with a muted effect on colors (especially on misty mornings), while late afternoon light has warm, reddish tones from the intensity of high ultraviolet light. Monet, in fact, used this changing light to special advantage, planting cool colors (blue and pink) on the east side of his garden and hot colors (yellows and reds) on the west side.

In order to create dramatic shadows, it may be necessary to clear obstructions from the edges of the property and to isolate tall trees. This usually requires the clearing of underbrush and the pruning of all low branches. Though the long shadows can look beautiful even on a flat section of lawn, the drama is heightened if the ground undulates. If you have a bare lot with nothing but lawn for a view, plant some fast-growing trees at opposite sides for the shadow effects. Some fast-growing hardy trees to consider are tulip poplars, dawn redwood, and river birch. For milder areas, consider eucalyptus and Italian stone pines. In southern California and southern Florida, make it palms.

Formal Shade Gardens

The most popular design for a formal shade garden is a sunken garden, whether the shade derives from city structures or woodland trees. The sunken part of the design adds dramatic height to surrounding walls or trees and produces a feeling of sheltered comfort.

Though sunken shade gardens are generally rectangular, they can be circular, taking on the aspect of an amphitheater with a central area for staging theatrical and musical events. The amphitheater can also serve as an exedra, a place for communal meetings with seats arranged in a semicircle. Since exedras date from ancient Greek and Roman times, they can take the form of ruins with columns and busts of Greek and Roman deities around the perimeter.

Formal shade gardens can be colorful, cheerful places where flowering plants like impatiens and tuberous begonias grow in abundance. On the other hand, you can make them look mysterious or even sinister by growing dark ivy on ruined walls and pedestals and by training snakelike grapevines and sinuous wisteria up columns and into the leaf canopy.

A formal sunken shade garden at Caramoor Estate, New York, uses wax begonias in a riot of colors for floral interest. Tall terra-cotta urns and a stone bust provide strong structural contrast.

Formal shade gardens may feature reflecting pools as well as shelters like grottoes, temples-of-love, and other Romantic architectural features known as follies.

Rhododendron and Azalea Gardens

Rhododendrons and azaleas go well together because they are from the same genus, *Rhododendron*. The only difference is that the former tend to have large leaves, large flowers held in trusses, and a billowing treelike habit, while the latter are more compact and bushy with smaller leaves and flowers. Also, azaleas tend to be easier to grow, surviving stressful conditions like drought and freezing temperatures that can kill rhododendrons. Even so, you may combine the two in shady gardens for a stunning display of color. A gently sloping shaded hillside overlooking a pond or stream will particularly satisfy their liking for good drainage and cool conditions.

Many species of azalea and rhododendron are native to North America, mostly to the Appalachian Mountains. These native azaleas tend to be deciduous, losing their leaves in winter, and many are highly fragrant. It's possible to create a very beautiful spring garden by planting only indigenous species like orange-flowered *R. calendulaceum*, pink-flowered *R. nudiflorum*, also known as *R. periclymenoides,* and yellow-flowered *R. austrinum*. British plant breeders have used many of these natives to hybridize the beautiful 'Exbury' strain of fragrant azaleas, which are predominantly yellow and orange. Unfortunately, the 'Exbury' strain is susceptible to mildew in many parts of North America.

The frothy flowers of foamflower and a cream-colored rhododendron combine with bluebells for an appealing color harmony along a woodland path.

Evergreen azaleas come mostly from Asia. They are rich in red, pink, and lavender shades as well as white. The two groups, evergreen and deciduous, should be kept apart because their colors tend to clash.

An advantage of azaleas is that some varieties do well in southern climates. Indeed, southern azaleas have made gardens like Callaway (south of Atlanta) and Magnolia Plantation (south of Charleston) world-famous. Planted beneath towering loblolly pines, the pastel-colored azaleas look spectacular reflected in garden lakes.

At Cedaridge Farm, our Azalea Hill does not try to compete with the kaleidoscopic color of Magnolia Plantation but concentrates instead on one

dominant hue: lavender. We planted the azalea variety 'Herbert', along with pink dog-woods and rosy redbuds. These bloom at the same time and present an unusual mono-chromatic theme in shades of pink, with touches of blue from Spanish bluebells planted at their feet.

The Flaming Forest of Joe Gable

The late Joseph B. Gable was a Pennsylvania farmer who devoted his life to breeding hardy varieties of evergreen flowering azaleas as well as some rhododendrons. His most fa-mous plant introduction was the azalea 'Stewartstonian', an orange-red variety named for

Stewartstown, the village where he lived. A colorful photo feature in *The Saturday Evening Post*, titled "The Flaming Forest of Joe Gable," pro-pelled Joe from obscurity to overnight fame. The story describes how he bred azaleas beneath a grove of trees on his property and how, in the spring, they looked like a forest fire blazing through the undergrowth.

Create your own flaming forest by mixing 'Stewartstonian' azaleas with burning bush. The azaleas will provide the forest-fire ef-fect in spring, and the burning bush will do it in autumn with its red leaves. Though burning bush produces its deepest red autumn coloring when planted in sun, shade imbues the leaves with spectacular pink tones.

City Shade Gardens

Cities are difficult places to garden at the best of times. Pollution can be lethal to many shade-loving plants, especially trees such as white birches, dogwoods, and maples. Also, tall buildings can keep courtyards and small city plots in a state of per-manent shade. If there is any soil with which to work, it is likely to be rock hard and filled with builder's debris and trash.

Shade-tolerant camellias and azaleas planted around an intimate seating area re-create the feeling of a woodland clearing in this charming city garden.

Passageways running between houses can be narrow and challenging to landscape. They can be dark and dank, with so little room to spread out that the only solution is to grow upward using hanging baskets, window box planters, and walls on which to support a trellis for growing espaliered trees, shrubs, and vines.

City plots have one big advantage. Even in northern locations, they can be sheltered from cold winds and retain heat so well during winter that it's possible to be adventurous with marginally hardy plants such as camellias in a New York City courtyard. Moreover, pests and diseases may not be as prevalent in the city as in country gardens.

Since most city backyards are rectangular in shape, they are ideal for formal gardens. In particular, sunken designs and plans with pronounced lines of perspective work well because they make the garden's limited space look larger than it really is. An easy illusion for making space look larger is to install a mirror at the end of the property so that the garden is reflected in it, doubling the apparent depth. Another simple effect is to install a facade of trelliswork at the bottom of the garden, using exaggerated lines of perspective to frame a wall mural of a landscape feature. The mural can be painted in a realistic style to simulate dramatic natural environments, such as a placid lakeside scene or a hazy seascape.

To increase light reflectivity in city gardens, consider painting walls or fences white. Place tall white trelliswork against high walls for vines to climb, thus extending foliage interest well above eye level. Some particularly good vines for cities are trumpet creeper (*Campsis radicans*), wisteria, and Virginia creeper (*Parthenocissus quinquefolia*), which has the additional advantage of beautiful red autumn coloring.

Take advantage of every window and balcony overlooking the garden space to trail cascading plants down into the garden, especially periwinkle (*Vinca minor*) and English ivy. For city gardens with no soil—just brick and concrete—consider growing shade plants in containers.

Container Shade Gardens

One of my most treasured memories of a trip to Nice in the South of France was exploring the quaint, shadowy, winding streets of old Antibes and finding a row house brimming with flowering plants. The owners had not only hung a window box on every window, they had also made special shelves and brackets for hanging clay planters and baskets. The home dripped plants from roof to street level.

Of course, the natural light of Antibes in summer is intense because of its proximity to the Mediterranean Sea. Even though the walls were shaded for most of the day, the plantings' height coupled with the light-colored stucco walls provided sufficient light for a wide array of flowering plants. The fact that the apartment fronted on the street and that the owners had not a scrap of ground in which to garden had not prevented their enjoyment of a Garden of Eden through the clever use of containers.

Shady decks, patios, and balconies are all good places to maintain a container garden, whether you decide to grow one spectacular plant in a wooden tub or to make a clever arrangement of containers in all shapes, textures, and sizes. In fact, an unshaded deck or patio can be so hot and uncomfortable that you might want to convert it to a shady site by erecting over it a simple lath structure. From the roof of the lath structure you can hang basket plants like fuchsias, and up the supports you can grow vines like table grapes. The base beneath a lath house is not only a good place to grow outdoor plants, it can be a good summer home for houseplants that need rejuvenation from a long winter of living indoors.

Though just about any plant can be grown in a container, it makes sense to choose plants that can bloom a long time. Especially suitable are shade-loving annuals like impatiens and coleus, as well as some everlasting summer-flowering bulbs like caladiums and tuberous begonias, which provide continuous color from summer to autumn frosts. Since small containers are prone to drying out too quickly, it pays to provide as big and deep a container as possible for your plants. Containers should have drainage holes and a drip tray to catch water runoff. Moreover, it's important to match the soil to the plant. Tuberous begonias, for example, like a humus-rich peat-based potting soil, while tulips and daffodils prefer a sandy growing medium. These mixes can be purchased from garden centers, but if you are planning to use a lot of containers, it is much more economical to make your own, using a blend of peat, sand, and garden topsoil. Moisture-holding granules like perlite are also good to mix in, as these provide aeration.

Above all, avoid plastic and metal containers. If sun strikes them at any part of the day, they can heat up rapidly and dehydrate plants fast. Much better container materials are wood or clay, especially those shaped like a whiskey half-barrel, with 25 to 30 gallons (95 to 113L) of soil capacity. These are roomy enough to hold a wide assortment of plants. Each barrel can be planted like a miniature garden, using small trees like Japanese maples for height and cascading foliage plants like spider plants to trail down the edges. For hanging baskets, buy wire holders that accommodate a nest of absorbent sphagnum moss or coco matting. These have good moisture-holding ability and allow plants to be pushed in at the edges for a complete cover of flowers or foliage. Attractive mulches of cocoa hulls or finely shredded leaves are also good for covering the soil surface to retain moisture.

Watering should be done whenever the soil surface feels dry. This may mean at least once a day in the case of hanging baskets that are prone to rapid drying out. The best tool for watering is a long-handled watering wand, since it allows you to poke the nozzle in between leaves and apply moisture directly to the soil. Fertilizing should be done at regular intervals. If you do not use a time-release fertilizer like Osmocote, which releases nutrients slowly over several months, use a diluted liquid solution every two weeks at the time of watering.

This assortment of flowering annuals is shaded nearly all day, but the height of the planting, good air circulation, and a warm climate encourage spectacular flowering.

Shade Plants
of Distinction

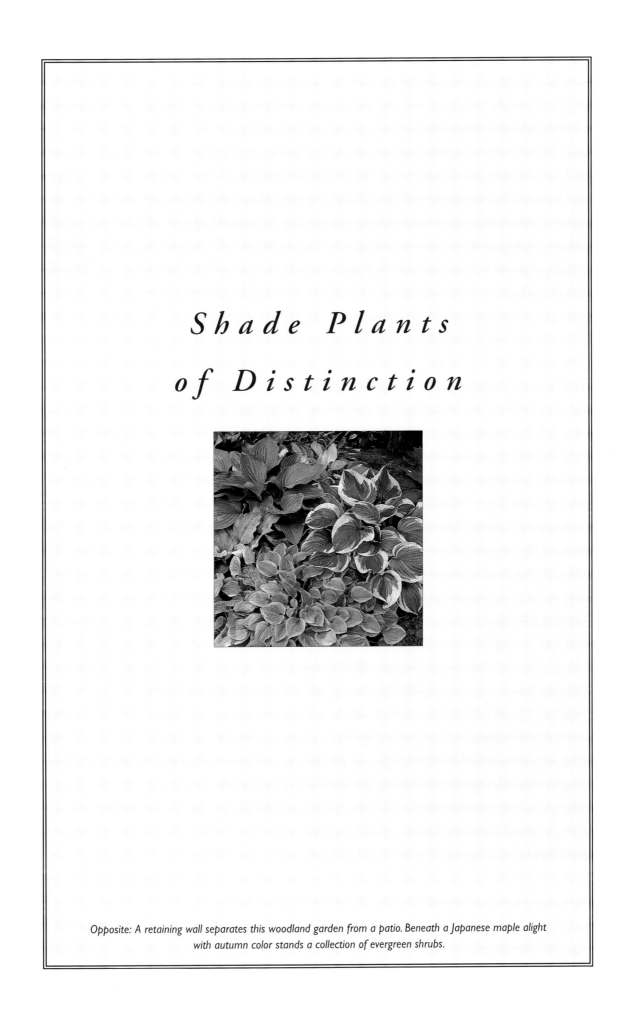

Opposite: A retaining wall separates this woodland garden from a patio. Beneath a Japanese maple alight
with autumn color stands a collection of evergreen shrubs.

The following selection of plants is not meant to be all-inclusive. Most are hardy perennials or woody plants, but a few are tender annuals or flowering bulbs that have special benefits in shade, such as a long period of floral color or attractive foliage. This list reflects my own personal favorites. The selection covers the three main shade classifications: light, medium, and deep shade.

Plant heights given are approximate and may vary according to light intensity, soil fertility, and other growth factors. If a particularly desirable variety exists, it is highlighted in the text. In selecting photographs I have steered away from featuring close-ups to showing mostly an overall view of the plant. In many cases I photographed a recommended use for the plant, such as an edging, a groundcover, or a slope cover. Many of these were taken at my home, Cedaridge Farm.

Acanthus mollis
(*bear's breeches*)

Bear's breeches, wonderful perennial plants, contrast dramatically with trees displaying light-colored bark, such as melaleuca.

The ancient Greeks used the leaf pattern of this tender perennial plant to adorn the tops of columns for their temples, for it has a large, lustrous, heavily indented, curling form. Its true beauty, however, is realized when it produces straight, blue-and-white flower spikes up to 4 feet (1.2m) high and 5 inches (12.5cm) wide for several weeks in summer. Although bear's breeches do well in full sun, especially in coastal locations, they also tolerate light shade. A hardier species, *A. spinossus*, has equally tall flower spikes, but the leaves are not as handsome. They are smaller, deeply serrated, and look more like a thistle. *A. mollis* prefers to grow in areas where the ground is not subjected to repeated thawing and freezing, while *A. spinossus* is more widely adapted.

The bold leaves of bear's breeches make a handsome contrast with other more graceful leaf forms, such as maidenhair ferns and hakone grass. The leaves are especially beautiful among white birch and paperbark trees (*Melaleuca linariifolia*). Bear's breeches are drought-resistant and tolerate poor sandy soils, but they flower best in well-drained, fertile loam. They are propagated from seed and root division.

Adiantum pedatum

(*m a i d e n h a i r   f e r n*)

Native to the Appalachian Mountains of North America, this extremely graceful hardy fern is slow-growing in its juvenile years. It is one of the most shade-tolerant ferns, growing even in deep shade. Dying down in winter, its soft-textured, light green fronds break dormancy in spring, unfurling to present a beautiful fan arrangement of leaflets on wiry black stems. Plants grow to 3 feet (90cm) high, spreading by underground stolons to form a vigorous colony. Besides shade, their most important need is cool soil, especially one receiving spray from a splashing waterfall or from regular amounts of moisture.

Use maidenhair ferns with violets, hostas, and European ginger along woodland walks and among boulders in shady rock gardens. The fronds are prized by florists for adding a delicate green accent to flower arrangements. They are propagated by spore culture and by division.

In company with hostas, Christmas fern, and white violets, the beautiful, layered fronds of maidenhair fern create a sensational foliage accent in a shady corner.

Aegopodium podagraria 'Variegata'

(variegated bishop's weed)

Variegated bishop's weed is available with white or gold edging. Here, the white leaf form makes a good weed-suffocating groundcover, especially when its delicate, lacy white flowers are in bloom.

The common form of bishop's weed has plain green leaves, lacks ornamental value, and is too aggressive for most garden situations. But the silver and gold variegated forms are not only beautiful, they are well behaved and stay within bounds. Though the plants produce white flower clusters in spring that resemble Queen Anne's lace, they are principally grown for the brightness of their ivy-shaped, serrated leaves and low, spreading habit.

Variegated bishop's weed is especially useful for growing as a low groundcover along a shady path, to edge a house foundation, or to make a dense mat effect around trees. Use it in combination with other spreading groundcovers such as yellow archangel, hellebores, vinca, English ivy, and ferns. The hardy perennial plants grow to 15 inches (37.5cm) high, die down in winter, and thrive in a wide range of soils, including poor soil. Plants tolerate light, medium, and even deep shade. They are easily propagated by division.

Ajuga reptans

(*b u g l e w e e d*)

There are many varieties of bugleweed from which to choose, including white, pink, and blue flowering kinds with lustrous, dark green, ruffled leaves arranged in a rosette. Some have bicolored and tricolored evergreen leaves, though these variegated forms tend to be weak-flowering. One of the best flowering varieties is 'Botanical Wonder', a medium blue with a 6-inch (15cm) -tall flower spike shaped like a candle. Ajugas are spreading plants and tolerate light to deep shade, though flowering tends to be sparse in deep shade. Provided that drainage is good, they are not fussy about soil, though they flower best in a humus-rich loam or sandy soil.

Above: A mass planting of bugleweed looks stunning in combination with lady ferns. The blue flowers of bugleweed are enhanced by lustrous evergreen leaves. Below: Dense plantings of lady's mantle are excellent for edging ponds and covering shady slopes, especially when the arching flower stems can dip onto a path, softening its edges.

Bugleweed can spread quickly by underground stolons and self-seeds into lawns, where it tends to look weedy. Plant it only where you want an aggressive plant that will take over the space. It is an eyecatching spring flower that looks sensational planted among pink bleeding hearts, columbine, and azaleas. Bugleweed is easily propagated by division after flowering.

Alchemilla mollis

(*l a d y ' s   m a n t l e*)

This hardy perennial is versatile in lightly shaded places, since its gray-green, ivy-shaped leaves provide a useful foil for other plants. In late spring, clouds of lime green flower clusters cover the foliage, lasting 4 weeks or more. The cushion-shaped plants grow up to 2 feet

(60cm) high and spread twice as wide. Give lady's mantle a humus-rich, moist soil. If your soil tends to turn dry in summer, mulch the plant with shredded leaves to maintain soil moisture.

Use lady's mantle as an edging along shady paths, as a groundcover to encircle trees, or among shady pondside plantings. The leaves have a soft, velvety texture and bead up moisture, so after rain or morning dew they sparkle like diamonds. Propagate by division after flowering.

Anemone nemerosa

(*w o o d   a n e m o n e*)

The low-growing, starry flowers and mounding habit of wood anemone make this plant excellent for the front of the shady border or the edge of a woodland path.

There are many kinds of anemone suitable for light to medium shade, but none so cheerful as this. A hardy perennial plant, it grows low, compact mounds of indented green leaves, up to 8 inches (20cm) high and covered with 2-inch (5cm) star-shaped white flowers. There is also a light pink form. Wood anemone is particularly beautiful in company with primroses, violets, and bluebells.

Another good anemone species to grow with the wood anemone is the Grecian windflower (*A. blanda*). Planted from bulbs, it flowers at about the same time, producing white, blue, or pink star-shaped flowers that grow close to the soil ahead of the leaves. Grecian windflowers are best for naturalizing under trees, while wood anemones are more appropriate as an edging to shady beds and borders and along woodland paths. Plants prefer a humus-rich, well-drained, loam soil. Mulch around roots with shredded leaves or pine needles to keep soil cool. Propagate by division after flowering.

Aquilegia canadensis

(wild columbine)

Wild columbine produces its masses of red flowers in early spring, here seen in company with bugleweed.

Many species and hybrids of perennial columbine are suitable for shade. *A. canadensis* is an American native capable of producing an extraordinary number of perky nodding red flowers on 2½-foot (75cm)-tall stems among indented cloverlike leaves. The bright yellow version, 'Corbett', looks good planted as a colony, creating what appears to be a pool of sunlight.

From the Rocky Mountains comes the beautiful sky blue columbine, *A. alpina*, while from Europe come a host of varieties developed from *A. vulgaris*, the best of which is 'Nora Barlow', a double-flowered, red-and-white bicolor. 'McKana's Giants' are a special large-flowered strain available in a wide color range, including red, white, blue, pink, yellow, and bicolors. Developed by an American home gardener and winner of an All-America award, it flowers the first year as an annual if seed is started 8 to 10 weeks before outdoor planting.

Columbine likes a humus-rich loam or sandy soil and good drainage. Most prefer a lightly shaded location, but *A. canadensis* tolerates medium shade. Propagate columbine by seed sown in the summer before flowering. Though classified as a perennial, it is usually not long-lived but continually self-seeds.

Asarum europaeum

(european ginger)

North America has two closely related wild gingers suited to shade gardens—*Asarum canadense* on the East Coast and *A. caudatum* on the West Coast. Both are deciduous and similar in appearance, producing handsome, heart-shaped leaves. European ginger, on the other hand, is evergreen and more ornamental, with larger, heart-shaped, lustrous leaves. Small, reddish brown, boat-shaped flowers, hidden beneath the leaves, appear in spring for pollination by slugs and snails. Plants thrive in light to deep shade and require good drainage and a humus-rich loam soil. Mulch plants with shredded leaves to keep the soil cool.

European ginger grows to 12 inches (30cm) high and spreads twice as wide. Use as a groundcover and for edging shady paths, especially in company with hostas and ferns. At Cedaridge Farm we also grow clumps between flagstone stepping-stones. Propagate *A. europaeum* by division in spring or late summer.

The lustrous, dark green, heart-shaped leaves of European ginger make an attractive groundcover even in deep shade. Plants remain evergreen in sheltered spots and where winters are mild. Purple boat-shaped flowers are hidden beneath the leaves.

Astilbe × arendsii

(false goatsbeard)

At Cedaridge Farm, hybrid astilbes are a required plant that we feature every year and add to every spring, especially along lightly shady parts of our stream and pond. We use them in the company of Japanese irises, ligularias, ostrich ferns, and hostas. Our favorite cultivar is 'Fanal', a deep red version developed by the late Georg Arends, a German perennial plant breeder. Other colors also include various shades of pink and purple as well as white.

These hardy perennials grow to 3 feet (90cm) high, displaying fernlike leaves that die down in winter and are sometimes bronze or green, depending on the variety. The species *A. chinensis* is a good dwarf form that grows to just 18 inches (45cm) high. Its light pink flowers are suitable for use as an edging or a groundcover. Astilbes prefer cool, moist, fertile, humus-rich soil. Propagate by division.

Above: The feathery flower plumes of false goatsbeard contrast with the smooth, broad, heart-shaped leaves of a blue-foliaged hosta. These unusual blooms help brighten a shady slope in late spring. **Below:** Tuberous begonias display a wide range of bold colors and large flowers against decorative foliage.

Begonia × tuberhybrida

(*tuberous begonia*)

All things considered, I doubt there is a more colorful family of flowers for shade than tuberous begonias. The color range includes yellow, orange, red, pink, white, and bicolors. Only a true blue is missing. Some of the flowers are enormous—up to 6 inches (15cm) across and fully doubled like a giant camellia blossom. Though tuberous begonias are tender flowering bulbs from tropical climates, the corms can be lifted after frost has killed the leaves and can be easily stored over winter in a dark, dry, frost-free place. Wash the corms of soil, allow to air-dry for two days, and nest in trays of peat. Around 6 to 8 weeks before the last frost in spring, they can be started in pots, covered with 2 inches (5cm) of soil, then transferred to the garden at a ready-to-bloom stage. They

will flower continuously all season, provided the soil is kept cool by mulching with shredded leaves or pine needles. The leaves are dark green, shaped like large ivy leaves. Flowering occurs in light to medium shade.

At Cedaridge Farm we use tuberous begonias in masses of mixed colors under trees and in hanging baskets and barrel planters. They demand a humus-rich, fertile, well-drained soil. Plants grow to 18 inches (45cm) high and combine well with caladiums, coleus, ferns, and impatiens. There is a hardy perennial form, *B. grandis*, that grows to 3 feet (90cm) high, with bright green leaves shaped like angels' wings. It produces clusters of airy pink flower sprays. Use it massed as a low hedge among shady paths.

Also, don't overlook the dwarf, 12-inch (30cm) wax begonia, *B.* × *semperflorens-cultorum* for light to medium shade. Grown as flowering annuals, wax begonias will remain in bloom for 10 weeks or more and are particularly suitable for creating ribbons of color.

Propagate hardy begonias by cuttings or division and tuberous begonias by corms, although the 'Nonstop' series can be grown from seed to flower in 10 weeks. Wax begonias are propagated from seed, requiring 10 weeks minimum to reach transplant size.

'Silverlight' is a beautiful, brightly colored hybrid variety of heartleaf that is best displayed massed in a woodland garden or as an edging for a shady path. The large, rounded leaves are evergreen.

Bergenia cordifolia

(*heartleaf*)

Noted for ruffled, lustrous, cabbagelike leaves and clusters of red, pink, lavender-purple, or white flowers held above the foliage, this hardy perennial flowers in early spring at the same time as tulips. In autumn its semievergreen leaves can change to orange and red. They look particularly beautiful against old brick or rough stone and planted beneath camellias. At Cedaridge Farm we can't grow camellias, so we plant heartleaf with early-flowering Lenten roses. A number of hybrids produced by the late Georg Arends, the German perennial breeder, are exceptionally beautiful, including 'Silver Light', which is white with a red eye, and 'Red Morning', which is a rosy red with a crimson eye.

Plants grow up to 2 feet (60cm) high and prefer light to deep shade and a moist, humus-rich, fertile soil. Mulch around plants with shredded leaves or pine needles to keep the soil cool and moisture-retentive. Use heartleaf as an edging to shady paths and water gardens, and massed to form a groundcover on moist slopes. Propagate by division.

Caladium ✕ hortulanum

(*rainbow plant*)

Sometimes called angel's wings or elephant ears, the preferred common name for caladiums in recent years is rainbow plant, which avoids confusion with other plants that bear the same common name.

Native to stream banks of South America, these tender flowering bulbs are grown for their decorative heart-shaped leaves, which are mostly red, pink, white, and many shades of green, with bicolor and tricolor combinations. They remain decorative all summer until autumn frost, sometimes producing an inconspicuous hooded white flower beneath the leaves. Florida is now the center for caladium production and hybridizing. Some of the best varieties include 'Rosebud' (green and white with pink veins), 'Freida Hemple' (red, maroon, and green), and 'White Queen' (white with red leaf veins). At Cedaridge Farm we always have a mass planting of rainbow plants encircling a tree and interspersed with orange impatiens. We also grow them in containers, several varieties to a barrel planter, so that the planting truly resembles a rainbow.

Plants grow to 3 feet (90cm) high and prefer light to medium shade, but survive even deep shade. Plant the bulbs in spring after all danger of frost, covering with 2 to 3 inches (5 to 7.5cm) of humus-rich, fertile soil. They are heat-tolerant and will survive boggy soil conditions. After frost kills the tops in autumn, lift the bulbs and store through winter in a dark, dry place at room temperature. The bulbs will rot if not kept warm and dry. Propagate by division of the bulbs.

Camellia japonica

(Japanese camellia)

This classic planting of camellias shows them tucked beneath the spreading branches of canyon oak trees.

Though the buds of camellias are tender to frost, plants are reliably hardy on the West Coast into Canada and in the Northeast as far as Washington, D.C. They can be grown further north in the shelter of courtyards. The flowers are circular, the petals arranged symmetrically in several layers around a powdery crown of yellow stamens. The evergreen leaves are oval, lustrous, and dark green. *C. japonica* blooms in early spring, while a similar species, *C. sasanqua*, is autumn-blooming. Colors include all shades of red and pink as well as white. There is also a rare yellow form, *C. lutea*, but it is small-flowered. We cannot grow camellias at Cedaridge Farm, though we frequently visit Magnolia Plantation near Charleston, South Carolina, to see a large pink variety that grew from seed and is registered with the American Camellia Society under the cultivar name 'Derek Fell'.

Plants grow to 15 feet (4.5m) high with an equal spread. They prefer light to medium shade, especially under a high tree canopy, and a well-drained, humus-rich loam or sandy soil. In northern gardens it is advisable to grow camellias in containers, such as wooden box-shaped planters that can be moved indoors during severe freezing weather. Good companions include early-flowering azaleas, ferns, and Lady Banks roses (*Rosa banksiae* var. *banksiae*). Propagate by tip cuttings after flowering.

Native to the Appalachian Mountains, this ground-hugging hardy perennial produces a dense mass of heart-shaped green leaves and a profusion of cheerful, yellow, star-shaped flowers.

Chrysogonum virginianum

(goldenstar)

New goldenstar cultivars flower generously in spring and intermittently through summer, and have a final flush of bloom in autumn before going dormant. Growing no more than 4 inches (10cm) high, the plants spread to several feet in one season. They are perfect for creating a carpetlike groundcover along woodland paths and encircling trees.

Plants grow in light to medium shade and prefer a humus-rich, well-drained soil. Use them in company with other groundcover plants such as periwinkle, European ginger, and primroses. At Cedaridge Farm we plant them beneath azaleas along woodland paths. Propagate by division in spring or late summer.

The goldenstar cultivar 'Allen Viette' blooms in spring and intermittently all summer.

Clivia miniata
(Kruger lily)

Tender Kruger lilies will thrive indoors in low-light situations, and actually enjoy being pot-bound.

Though these early-flowering bulbs are tender, they are very popular shade-loving plants for frost-free areas of North America such as southern Florida and southern California. In northern gardens they are good to grow in pots in low-light situations, flowering in early spring. (Recently at an auction, the bulb of a yellow variety was sold for $1,750 to a mail-order nursery, where it was promptly propagated and its bulbs offered for $500 each. Usually, bulbs sell for $10 each.) Kruger lilies produce a cluster of orange trumpet-shaped florets that can measure 10 inches (25cm) across. Even a small colony of these plants looks sensational beneath live oaks, tree ferns, and palms in the company of ground ferns.

Plants grow to 3 feet (90cm) high, tolerate light to medium shade, and prefer a humus-rich, well-drained loam or sandy soil. They especially like their roots to be pot-bound or confined by boulders. At Cedaridge Farm we grow Kruger lilies in a shaded conservatory as a houseplant with amaryllis, which blooms at the same time. Propagate by bulb division.

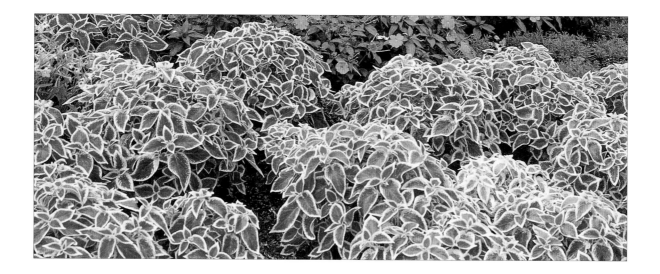

Coleus blumei
(*flame nettle*)

Grown mostly as a tender annual, coleus is valued for its leaves, which come in a vast range of colors including red, orange, yellow, maroon, and lime green, plus bicolor and tricolor combinations of these. The leaf shape can be broad or slender, smooth or fringed, depending on variety. In late summer they produce weedy-looking blue flower spikes that are best removed to keep the plant looking neat and tidy. Indeed, the 'Saber' series has been specially bred to delay flowering into autumn so that frequent deadheading to keep the plants compact is not needed.

Coleus plants grow to 3 feet (90cm) high with an equal spread. They prefer light to medium shade and a humus-rich soil. Mulch around plants with shredded leaves or pine needles to keep the soil cool. New plants are mostly grown from seed started 8 to 10 weeks before planting outdoors after all danger of frost. Plants are also easily propagated from cuttings. Any branch tip will root in plain water.

The coleus cultivar known as 'Wizard' represents an improvement over older kinds, as it stays mounded and compact all summer.

Corydalis flexuosa 'Blue Panda'
(*blue bleeding heart*)

There are two species of *Corydalis* popular in shade gardens—*C. lutea* (yellow) and *C. flexuosa* (blue). They both resemble bleeding hearts, with their feathery foliage and clusters of tubular flowers. At Cedaridge Farm we have a bleeding heart garden that combines both *Corydalis* and *Dicentra* varieties for a highly attractive display. It is the blue, however, that brings gasps of admiration from visitors. In well-grown specimens, the mound-shaped plants (up to 18 inches [45cm] high) are covered with flowers the color of the sky.

'Blue Panda' was discovered growing along mountain streams in western China. In home gardens it demands a cool, moist, humus-rich, fertile soil. It is happiest in sheltered light shade, particularly beside water, where it can echo the color of a reflected blue sky. Mulch around the plants with shredded leaves or pine needles to keep the soil cool. Propagate by division.

Above: 'Blue Panda' is a new cultivar of a hardy perennial that is closely related to common bleeding heart. Below: Though this hardy cyclamen is growing persistently through a cover of ivy, it generally cannot compete with aggressive groundcovers. Note the beautiful marbled leaves.

Cyclamen hederifolium

(ivy-leaf cyclamen)

Also called fall cyclamen and baby cyclamen, these hardy perennial plants are perfect miniatures of the familiar florist's cyclamen (*C. persicum* hybrids), which are too tender for growing outdoors except in frost-free climates like southern California and southern Florida. The ivy-leaf cyclamen is autumn-flowering. It produces nodding flowers with swept-back petals and waxy, dark green, ivy-shaped leaves marbled with silver. Plant height is rarely more than 8 inches (20cm) with a spread of 12 inches (30cm), though plants increase from division of underground bulbs (corms) to create large colonies.

Ivy-leaf cyclamen thrives in light shade, especially in well-drained, humus-rich soil, where it will self-seed. Propagation is by division of corms and by seed sown 10 weeks before planting outdoors in spring after frost danger. Once established, plants are hardy, dying down after autumn frost.

Dicentra species
(bleeding heart)

Common bleeding heart displays masses of pendant, heart-shaped florets in early spring.

There is a native bleeding heart, *D. eximia*, indigenous to the Appalachian Mountains. This has been crossed with a species native to the Pacific Northwest, *D. formosa*, to produce an everblooming hybrid, 'Luxuriant'. These, and the common bleeding heart (*Dicentra spectabilis*), are good hardy perennials for growing in light- to medium-shaded locations. They like each other's company, which is how we use them at Cedaridge Farm. We also intersperse them among species of *Corydalis*, which are closely related and similar in appearance. Common bleeding heart is the taller, growing to 4 feet (1.2m). In early spring it produces arching stems laden with pendant, heart-shaped blooms that can be pink or white, depending on variety. The leaves are feathery and deeply indented.

All the bleeding hearts prefer a fertile, humus-rich soil. It is natural for their leaves to die down after flowering and for the roots to remain dormant through both summer drought and winter freezes. Propagation is by division.

Digitalis purpurea
(common foxglove)

A hardy biennial, common foxgloves make strong leafy growth their first year of life, then flower in spring the second season. They give the impression of being perennials by self-seeding to create self-perpetuating colonies. Though the plant is native to Europe, I never saw

Foxgloves in mixed colors decorate a shady slope at Cedaridge Farm.

common foxgloves growing more prolifically than in Oregon, where a Douglas fir forest had been clear-cut and hydroseeded with foxgloves. To see thousands of acres in full flower is an uplifting sight. Though they relish sunny spaces, they also thrive in lightly shaded locations, and we use thousands of them at Cedaridge Farm along woodland paths and clearings.

Plants grow to 5 feet (1.5m) high, producing velvety broad pointed leaves and erect flower stems studded with tubular flowers in red, pink, purple, apricot, yellow, and white. Propagate from seed. The annual variety, 'Foxy', will flower the first year from seed started indoors 8 to 10 weeks before outdoor planting.

Doronicum cordatum
(leopard's bane)

I have seen these growing wild in deep shade throughout Normandy, France, but they flower best in a light- to medium-shaded location. A hardy perennial, leopard's bane has shiny, ivy-shaped green leaves and bright yellow daisylike flowers up to 2 inches (5cm) across. The plants are spring-flowering, dying down after autumn frost. At Cedaridge Farm we use them in combination with wild blue phlox (*Phlox divaricata*) and Spanish bluebells for a stunning yellow-and-blue color harmony. Plants grow to 3 feet (90cm) high

The cheerful, yellow, daisylike flowers of leopard's bane appear in early spring, and make good companions for tulips.

and spread to form beautiful colonies, especially in a fertile, humus-rich soil with good drainage. Propagate by division after flowering and from seeds sown in summer.

Eranthis hyemalis
(winter aconite)

Winter aconites shrug off a light coating of snow to bloom extra early in the season.

Every sunny day in February I look to see which blooms first at Cedaridge Farm—winter aconites or snowdrops. Generally, the winter aconites are a day earlier, but the two mixed together make a glorious sight! What cheerful plants aconites are, blooming during intermittent thaws even before the last snowfalls of winter. If covered with snow after flowering, they simply wait patiently until the sun melts it away. The iridescent flowers resemble buttercups, appearing before the true leaves. Initially, the flowers grow 3 inches (7.5cm) high with a frilly green collar, but as the plants mature they make mounds of serrated leaves up to 8 inches (20cm) high.

These hardy perennial bulbs like to be grown in lightly shaded woodland under deciduous trees. They prefer a fertile, humus-rich loam or sandy soil. Aconites multiply freely from self-seeding if the leaf litter is free of weeds. Also, propagation is by division of the bulbs after flowering.

Fritillaria imperialis
(crown imperial)

One of the best places to display this stately hardy bulb is at the edge of woodland in light shade. Growing to 4 feet (1.2cm) high, the slender flowering stalks have lilylike pointed leaves up the stem, topped by a cluster of six nodding bell-shaped flowers beneath a crown of leaves. Plants bloom in early spring about the same time as late daffodils and early tulips. The leaves have a skunklike odor when bruised, making them objectionable to deer. Colors include orange and yellow. Crown imperial is related to guinea-hen flower (*F. meleagris*), which is also suitable for light shade, but guinea-hen flower has smaller bell-shaped flowers, grasslike leaves, and a checkered petal design.

Crown imperials prefer to have their flattened bulbs planted on their sides to avoid water collecting in a hollow on top of the bulb and rotting it. Give them a fertile, humus-rich, well-drained soil. Propagate by division of the bulbs.

Crown imperials shine at the edge of woodland, along with shimmering tulips. Well-drained slopes suit them best, as the bulbs are highly susceptible to rotting when planted in poorly drained soils.

Galium odoratum

(*sweet woodruff*)

The small, white flower clusters of this spreading groundcover appear for several weeks in late spring. A popular component of herb gardens, sweet woodruff is used to flavor German May wines. Its finely textured leaves are splayed out like a starburst and are highly ornamental, even after the flowers have faded. It tolerates even deep shade and can cover large expanses under trees. Sweet woodruff is not overly aggressive and can be easily confined by pulling it up at the edges. At Cedaridge Farm, we use it along woodland paths as part of tapestry gardens that rely on foliage textures for ornamental effect.

Sweet woodruff's dainty white flower clusters appear for several weeks in spring, though the starburst leaves continue until frost.

These hardy perennial plants grow just 6 inches (15cm) high. They can creep up and over boulders as long as the original planting is rooted in a humus-rich loam or sandy soil with good drainage. It is easily propagated by division of established clumps.

Hakonechloa macra
(hakone grass)

'Aureola' is a variegated form of Japanese hakone grass.

Native to Japan, this clump-forming hardy perennial grass spreads by underground roots but tends to be slow-growing. A variegated form, golden variegated hakone grass (*H. macra* 'Aureola'), has bright yellow foliage striped with green in summer. In autumn, however, its short, slender leaves turn deep ruddy pink. Though beautiful for edging shady paths, it also makes a sensational container plant. Small, inconspicuous yellow flowers appear in summer.

Plants grow to 12 inches (30cm) high and spread out in all directions like a dwarf bamboo, but they are never as invasive as bamboo. Hakone grass thrives in light to medium shade and prefers a fertile, humus-rich loam or sandy soil. Propagate by division and from seed sown in late summer and transplanted to the garden the following spring.

Hedera helix
(English ivy)

Many species of ivy are suitable for shady locations, some with leaves the size of dinner plates. One of the best is English ivy, a vining, hardy, woody plant that can be used as both a weed-suffocating groundcover and a climber. The pointed, indented leaves range in size from 1 to 4 inches (2.5 to 10cm) across, depending on variety. At Cedaridge Farm we use the cultivar 'Needlepoint' because its foliage is not as coarse as the species and, for contrast, 'Little Diamond', a white-and-green variegated form. We like to grow them up tree trunks to enhance uninteresting bark and over preformed molds of wire and branches to create topiary animals like deer.

English ivy will grow 100 feet (30m) high if it has support. Its sinuous stems have aerial roots that cling to porous stone or wooden surfaces with ease. It is tolerant of all kinds of shade, including deep shade, and the only difficult soil conditions for it are hard clay or standing water. Though slow-growing the first year, it creeps the next and leaps in subsequent seasons, often requiring vigorous pruning to keep it within bounds. Propagate by cuttings.

Common English ivy decorates a tree trunk along a woodland path.

Helleborus orientalis

(L e n t e n   r o s e)

There are many species of *Helleborus* suitable for shade, but the Lenten rose is the most widely adapted and the easiest to grow in light to medium shade. This hardy evergreen perennial has leathery leaves like pachysandra and, in early spring, masses of nodding, cup-shaped flowers in shades of red, pink, purple, and maroon as well as white. After fading, the flowers dry to shades of maroon and green. A crown of powdery yellow stamens at the center of each flower heightens the flowering display, which can last several months. At Cedaridge Farm we have large beds of Lenten roses growing under black walnut trees, which poison

Not a true rose, the Lenten rose is more closely related to buttercups. Lenten roses come in a mix of flower colors and have lustrous, leathery, evergreen leaves.

other plants. We started with fifty plants and now have thousands that have seeded themselves from the original colony.

Plants grow to 18 inches (45cm) high with an equal spread. They prefer a fertile, humus-rich loam or sandy soil. Mulch around the plants with shredded leaves to keep the soil cool. Plant Lenten roses close to winter aconites, ferns, and early azaleas for extra appeal. Propagate by seed or by transplanting small volunteer seedlings that will spring up around the mother plants.

Hemerocallis hybrids
(*d a y l i l i e s*)

Though daylilies are famous for their drought-tolerance in dry, sunny spaces, they thrive in light shade, producing beautiful trumpet-shaped blooms on long slender stems among arching, sword-shaped leaves. Colors include yellow, orange, apricot, red, lavender, cream, white, maroon, and bicolors. Some 'Siloam' hybrids are notable for their clear colors with contrasting dark zones around the throat. The dwarf daylily 'Stella d'Oro' (orange) and the taller 'Happy Returns' (yellow) are capable of flowering nonstop from late spring until autumn frost. Height ranges from 1 to 4 feet (30 to 120cm), depending on the variety. Some daylily flowers like 'Mary Todd' (yellow) are as big as amaryllis blooms.

The only condition presenting a problem for daylilies, which tolerate a wide range of soils, is permanently boggy

A mass of wayside daylilies has naturalized behind a garden bench. This site receives just 4 hours of sun a day.

soil. For best flowering, give them a humus-rich, fertile soil and good drainage. Use the dwarf everblooming varieties for containers. Propagate by division after flowering, though transplanting can be done at any time during spring, summer, or autumn.

Hesperis matronalis

(dame's rocket)

Related to phlox, these tall-growing plants produce in late spring tapering flower spikes crowded with four-petaled flowers in mostly white, pink, and rosy red. Native to the waysides and woodlands of North America, they are hardy biennials that produce a rosette of spear-shaped leaves the first season, then elongate into flower spikes 3 to 4 feet (90 to 120cm) high the second. At Cedaridge Farm we find them beautiful when planted among clumps of hostas and ferns, with a heavy emphasis on the white-flowered variety for a glittering appearance.

Once you have dame's rocket in your garden, you are likely to have it forever, since it sets large quantities of seed that will germinate wherever there is bare soil. However, they are not invasive plants. Even if they seed into places they shouldn't, they form a perfect partnership with everything that grows. Give them light to medium shade and a humus-rich loam or sandy soil. Start seeds mid-to late summer of the season prior to flowering.

Spires of dame's rocket add a twinkling quality to the shady edges of a path.

Hosta species and cultivars

(plantain lily)

A mixed planting of hostas surrounds the honey-colored bark of 'Heritage' river birches.

Thousands of varieties of hostas have been hybridized by crossing some forty species, largely native to Japan. The cultivar 'Frances Williams' is the most popular, perfectly suited to shade because its two-tone coloration (blue and lime green) enlivens dark areas better than the plain green- or blue-leaf varieties. Growing 2 feet (60cm) high with a 4-foot (1.2m) spread, this hardy perennial produces flower spikes of pale blue, bell-shaped flowers in early summer. After frost the leaves disappear, and the plant goes dormant until the return of warm weather in spring. At Cedaridge Farm we like to plant 'Frances Williams' in company with 'Royal Standard', which has fragrant white flowers the size of foxgloves and shiny, lime green leaves that also brighten shady areas.

Hostas are invaluable for creating tapestry gardens, where foliage effects alone are the main attraction. With leaves blistered like brocade, they are particularly dramatic planted adjacent to ferns and hakone grass. Give hostas light, medium, or deep shade and a fertile, humus-rich soil. Mulch around plants with shredded leaves to maintain a cool, moist soil. Propagate by division of three-year-old plants in spring or autumn.

Hydrangea macrophylla

(French hydrangea)

These hardy, deciduous, woody shrubs produce beautiful, heavily veined, spear-shaped leaves and globular flower heads—mopheads—that can be 10 inches (25cm) across. The color range includes red, pink, purple, blue, and white. In some varieties the coloration is affected by the type of soil they are grown in—blue tones in alkaline soil and pink in acid soil. Growers add lime for extra blue coloration and sulphur for the best pink. At Cedaridge Farm our favorites are 'Nikko Blue' and 'Europa' (pink). Lacecap hydrangeas have flattened flower heads and a lacelike appearance from a close concentration of flower buds in the center and a wide spacing of florets around the edges.

Hydrangeas grow to 10 feet (3m) high and lose their leaves in winter. Even if the top growth dies back in a severe winter, plants can grow new flowering stems the following season. They do well in light to medium shade as long as their roots stay cool. Give them a deep, fertile, humus-rich loam or sandy soil and mulch around the roots to maintain a cool, moist soil. Plant them as hedges along woodland paths and along the east or west side of a house foundation. Propagate by tip cuttings.

Lacecap hydrangea flowers along a woodland path in summer beside delicate ferns. These two plants offer a romantic touch that is often absent from shade gardens.

Impatiens wallerana
(patience plant)

There are basically two kinds of impatiens suitable for all kinds of shade—*I. wallerana* hybrids from South America, with flowers up to 2 inches (5cm) across, and *I.* 'New Guinea' hybrids, mostly derived from crosses with *I. hawkeri* from Indonesia. These have flowers up to 3 inches (7.5cm) across and leaves that may be bicolored or tricolored, depending on variety. Both are best grown as tender annuals, but *I. wallerana* hybrids are the most versatile, flowering profusely as low-mounded plants from spring until autumn frost. They are easily grown from seed, started indoors 8 to 10 weeks

The popular impatiens cultivar 'Accent', which boasts ever-blooming flowers, decorates a shady, fern-covered slope.

ahead of transplanting outside after all danger of frost. Favorite varieties at Cedaridge Farm include the 'Accent' series, which comes in many shades of red, pink, and lavender, plus white and bicolors. Plants grow to 12 inches (30cm), have a basal branching habit, and spread to 3 feet (90cm) wide by the end of the season. They are ideal for massing in shady beds and borders and for encircling trees.

'New Guinea' impatiens are shrubby in habit, grow 3 to 4 feet (90 to 120cm) tall, and flower more sparsely than *I. wallerana* but with larger flowers. The serrated, spear-shaped leaves of 'New Guinea' impatiens can also be highly ornamental. 'Tango' is a particularly popular cultivar because of its rich orange color.

Give impatiens a fertile, humus-rich loam or sandy soil, and mulch around the plants with shredded leaves to keep the soil moist and cool. Propagate *I. wallerana* from seed, *I. hawkeri* hybrids from cuttings.

Iris cristata
(crested iris)

Several varieties of iris tolerate light shade, including the Dutch iris (*I.* × *hollandica*), yellow flag iris (*I. pseudacorus*), and roof iris (*I. tectorum*), but the iris that flowers best in shade is undoubtedly the native crested iris, indigenous to the meadows and shady stream banks of the Appalachian Mountains. Plants are low-growing, just 4 inches (10cm) tall, with bright blue or pure white flowers. The blooms are 3 inches (7.5cm) across and shaped like small Dutch irises with broad, sword-shaped, blue-green leaves.

Crested irises can form large, creeping colonies beside woodland paths and on gentle slopes. They look beautiful partnered with yellow flowers such as goldenstar and pink flowers such as 'Rosea' creeping phlox. Give crested iris a humus-rich loam or sandy soil with good drainage and light to medium shade. Propagate by division of the rhizomes.

A colony of dainty blue dwarf crested iris covers a shady hill.

Kerria japonica
(Japanese kerria)

Above: Variegated kerria lights up a woodland floor in spring. Below: Yellow archangel is best known for its evergreen, silvery leaves, but it also boasts beautiful yellow flowers that bloom in spring.

The double-flowered golden yellow form of this hardy, woody, deciduous plant grows tall and gangly in shade, but the original species—with its single, canary yellow, roselike flowers—stays bushy and compact. It brightens shady places like an oasis of light. A cultivar with variegated leaves further enhances the brilliance of this spring-flowering shrub.

Plants grow to 6 feet (1.8m) tall but can be kept low and compact by shearing. They spread by stoloniferous roots to create a dense weave of branches covered with flowers in spring. At Cedaridge Farm we plant them beneath redbud trees to create a startling combination of yellow and rose pink. Give kerria light shade and a well-drained, humus-rich loam or sandy soil. Propagate by cuttings.

Lamium galeobdolon
(yellow archangel)

Another common name for this hardy perennial is dead nettle. It has a low-spreading growth habit and spear-shaped evergreen leaves with silver markings, which make it decorative all year. Its 4-inch (10cm) spires of lemon yellow blooms that appear in spring are a bonus. Plant in light to deep shade.

Plants grow to 4 inches (10cm) high and spread rapidly by creeping stolons. Silver-marked 'Herman's Pride' makes shorter clumps and is not as aggressive as the species. Yellow archangel is not, however, an overly aggressive plant and is easily confined by simply pulling it up at the edges. Use in company with other species of *Lamium*, especially *L. maculatum* 'White Nancy', which has white-centered leaves and white flowers, or 'Pink Pewter', which has white-centered leaves and pink flowers. Give them all a humus-rich, well-drained loam or sandy soil. Propagate by division of the stolons.

Ligularia stenocephala
(*r o c k e t   r a g w o r t*)

These are tall plants with big, serrated, ivy-shaped leaves and tapering spires of yellow flower clusters. The most common cultivar by far is 'The Rocket'. It is probably the most conspicuous flowering plant you can grow for medium to deep shade. Not suitable for small spaces or for planting singly, it is best used on moist, shady stream edges where it can form a sizable colony. Rocket ragwort looks good in the company of other large-leafed plants like hostas, goatsbeard, hydrangeas, and ostrich ferns.

Rocket ragwort produces its best flower spikes in a fertile, humus-rich, moist soil. Wilting of leaves is natural during noon heat.

If sun falls across the plants during the heat of the day, the leaves have an annoying tendency to wilt, but they perk up again when they feel relief from the sun and heat. Plants grow to 6 feet (1.8m) high and prefer a humus-rich, moist loam or sandy soil. Mulch around the plants with shredded leaves to help maintain a cool, moist soil. Propagation is by division.

Lilium 'Asiatic' hybrids
(*A s i a t i c   l i l i e s*)

The plant genus *Lilium* (garden lilies) is enormous, with wild species widely dispersed throughout the world. At one time they were all considered temperamental and sensitive to poor soil and disease. The late Jan de Graaff, an Oregon lily hybridizer, changed their reputation by breeding a race of hardy, easy-care lilies known as 'Asiatic Hybrids', using mostly wild species from China for parents. The most famous is the orange lily, 'Enchantment'. Though de Graaff named his best mixture 'Mid-Century', I often see it advertised as 'Enchantment Mixed' to capitalize on the 'Enchantment' reputation. Flower colors include red, yellow, orange, apricot, pink, maroon, and white. Most have handsome spots in the throat of each trumpet-shaped bloom. The plants stand about 3 feet (90cm) high the first year, 4 feet (1.2m) or more the second.

Given light shade and a fertile, humus-rich soil that drains well, the Asiatic lilies will multiply almost as freely as daffodils. Planting them with ferns and hostas enhances their beauty. Moreover, the stems of Asiatic lilies are long enough to cut for spectacular fresh flower arrangements. Propagate by division of the bulbs, which should be covered with 6 inches (15cm) of soil from the base of the bulb. The bulbs are composed of clovelike segments, each of which can produce a new plant.

Lobelia cardinalis

(cardinal flower)

Above: Among lilies, the Asiatic hybrids are the most vigorous and widely adapted. In well-drained, humus-rich soil they will easily establish large colonies. Below: Cardinal flowers grow in the moist soil along the bank of a shady pond.

When I first moved to Cedaridge Farm, I discovered wild colonies of cardinal flowers growing along our stream. All I needed to do to help them spread was to clear away the weeds and brambles threatening to suffocate them. Now they are a main feature of our summer floral display, and, as a bonus, they attract hummingbirds. When I find them seeded into odd corners of the property, I move them into shaded parts of the main garden. The flowers are composed of butterfly-shaped florets that create a spire. Plants grow 4 feet (1.2m) high and form a rosette of evergreen spear-shaped leaves. There is a closely related blue species, *L. syphilitica*, which blooms at the same time.

Provide cardinal flowers with a humus-rich, moist soil in light shade. Mulch around the roots to keep them cool. Cardinal flowers will even tolerate long periods of being covered with shallow water. Propagate by seed sown in summer the season before flowering and by division.

Lunaria annua
(*money plant*)

Variegated money plant brightens up a woodland garden. Its purple flowers are followed by silvery seed pods.

Popular at Thanksgiving for decorating dried flower arrangements, the seedpods of this hardy biennial look like silver dollars when dried. Few people realize that in spring before the pods develop, the plant produces sprays of purple flowers, especially in light to medium shade. There is also a white-flowered cultivar and a particularly attractive form with variegated leaves. Its serrated, heart-shaped leaves have a conspicuous white edging that presents a more sophisticated accent in woodland than the common form.

Plants grow to 3 feet (90cm) high, flowering in early spring at about the same time as tulips. The plants are best propagated from seed started in the summer of the season before flowering. Being biennial, the flowers occur in the second season and then die. If, however, you save the seeds inside the silvery pods, broadcast them over bare soil, and rake them in, you need never be without money plant since it reseeds itself so easily. Give money plant a humus-rich loam or sandy soil with good drainage. Seeds may also be purchased from seed racks in garden centers.

Mertensia virginica
(*Virginia bluebell*)

Native to deciduous woodlands throughout the northeastern United States, Virginia bluebells are early spring-flowering plants that thrive in light or dappled shade and are capable of colonizing large stretches of woodland. The clump-forming plants grow to 2 feet (60cm) high, producing fleshy oval green leaves and clusters of blue, bell-shaped flowers held above the foliage. There is also a rare white form. These hardy perennial plants go dormant during summer heat and winter freezes. They are good companions for trilliums, Spanish bluebells, and pink bleeding hearts.

Suitable for light to medium shade, Virginia bluebells prefer a humus-rich loam or sandy soil and good drainage. Propagated by division, the divided roots sometimes remain dormant for a whole year before sprouting. Where they have bare soil to seed into, they readily self-seed.

Above: Virginia bluebells can colonize vast areas of woodland. Below: The best way to use blue forget-me-nots is to mass them along paths in light shade. White and pink forms also exist.

Myosotis alpestris

(forget - me - not)

The benefit of using forget-me-nots in shady places is their ability to create vast stretches of blue mist with their small blue flowers that last a month or more, beginning in early spring. They look lovely massed along woodland paths and around trees with primroses in light or dappled shade. Use them also around pink bleeding hearts for a pretty pink-and-blue color harmony. In addition to the blue, there are also pink and white forms.

Plants grow 12 inches (30cm) high and equally wide. They are hardy biennials, mostly grown from seed started in summer the year before flowering. They tolerate a wide range of soils, but do best in a moist, cool, humus-rich loam or sandy soil. Once you have forget-me-nots in your garden you are likely to see them self-seeding into any places with bare soil. However, they are not invasive and look good with any other shade-loving flowers.

Narcissus hybrids
(*d a f f o d i l s*)

A naturalized planting of daffodils grows beneath deciduous trees at Colonial Williamsburg in Virginia.

Though daffodils are often seen flowering in woodlands, they must have sufficient light to ripen their foliage so that they can recharge their bulbs and repeat their flowering performance the following spring. They do best in glades where the overhead leaf canopy has been thinned and in deciduous woodland with dappled shade. There are many hardy daffodils from which to choose. At Cedaridge Farm some of our favorites are 'Fortissima' (a large variety of trumpet daffodil) and the fragrant 'Pheasant's Eye' (which has white flowers and a small green cup with red frill).

Daffodils grow 6 to 12 inches (15 to 30cm) high, depending on the variety. Some are cluster-flowered, and all are suitable for fresh flower arrangements. They look beautiful partnered with blue squill, blue grape hyacinths, and primroses. Give them a humus-rich soil and good drainage. At Cedaridge Farm we grow more daffodils than anything else, massing them at the edge of woodland, on the border of lawns, and along shady sections of our stream. They are easily propagated by dividing the bulbs in summer after the leaves have died down. Always plant daffodil bulbs in late summer or early autumn, though planting can continue as late as Christmas if the ground is not frozen.

Paeonia hybrids
(*p e o n i e s*)

Both the herbaceous peony and the tree peony have been hybridized to produce many beautiful varieties, all of which thrive in lightly shaded locations. Herbaceous peonies are mostly hybrids of *P. officinalis*, hardy perennials that grow to 3½ feet (105cm) high and bloom in late spring. They like a prolonged cold spell during winter in order to bloom well. Tree peonies, on the other hand, are hybrids of *P. suffruticosa*, woody shrublike plants that bloom earlier than herbaceous peonies. They also grow taller—up to 10 feet (3m) high—and do not need such cold winters.

At Cedaridge Farm we grow them both. Our favorite herbaceous peony is 'Bowl of Beauty', a cup-shaped, deep pink variety with a powdery crown of yellow stamens. Our favorite tree peony is 'Joseph Rock' for its creamy white petals and maroon petal markings reminiscent of an Oriental poppy. The color range of both kinds includes

The herbaceous peony 'Bowl of Beauty' shows off its alluring cup-shaped blooms and handsome yellow stamens.

red, pink, and white. For tree peonies it also includes yellow and apricot tones.

Give all peonies a fertile, humus-rich, well-drained loam soil. Herbaceous peonies often die down and go dormant through summer heat and winter freezes. Tree peonies lose their leaves, but the woody branches, studded with fat buds, remain aboveground. Propagate by root divisions made in late summer. Tree peonies can also be increased by tip cuttings taken in late summer.

Phlox stolonifera
(c r e e p i n g   p h l o x)

Most varieties of phlox tolerate light shade. Some of the early spring-flowering kinds like *P. stolonifera* and *P. divaricata* (Canadian creeping phlox) will even tolerate a medium-shaded location. These two species are hard to tell apart. They flower together and are rich in pink and blue shades, particularly sky blue, violet-blue, deep pink, and white. Both kinds grow to just 10 inches (25cm) high. They have rounded, glossy green leaves and a spreading ground-hugging habit that is not invasive. 'London Grove', a variety of *P. divaricata*, is sensational, with fragrant flowers and a shimmering violet-blue color. *P. stolonifera* 'Blue Ridge' is the best blue form, while 'Variegata' is a sensational pink with the added bonus of creamy white foliage. For a really sensational carpeting effect, grow them all

in merging drifts with patches of foam-flower. In woodland gardens you simply cannot have enough of these stunning native North American wildflowers, especially in dappled shade among clumps of azaleas.

These species of creeping phlox like to grow in a humus-rich loam or sandy soil with good drainage. They are easily propagated by division after flowering and readily self-seed into bare soil.

Above: Blue creeping phlox partnered with pink bleeding heart, money plant, and hostas ornament a bed that uses stones to raise the soil level around a tree. Below: 'Barnhaven' primroses grow serenely among the roots of an ash tree at Cedaridge Farm.

Primula × polyantha

(Barnhaven primrose)

If there is one plant at Cedaridge Farm that I would sacrifice everything else to keep, it is the 'Barnhaven' strain of hardy hybrid primroses. Developed from species mostly native to Europe, this strain comprises about forty cultivars hybridized over a period of forty years by Mrs. Florence Levy (née Bellis). An American concert pianist, Mrs. Levy devoted her spare time to breeding the finest primroses the world has ever seen at her home near Portland, Oregon. When Mrs. Levy retired, she passed her stock plants on to a British nursery, which in turn entrusted the stocks to a grower in Brittany, France.

Though there are larger flowering varieties like the 'Pacific Giants', I like the 'Barnhavens' because of their old-fashioned appearance, subtle colors, and hardiness. Not only are the familiar yellow, red, white, and blue colors present but also apricot, pink, and mahogany—many with a gold edge to the petals. Some of the best are also fully double. The plants form rosettes of bright green or dark green leaves with prominent leaf veins and a blistered texture. Though all the 'Barnhavens' divide readily, they are easily grown from seed started in spring or early summer of the year before flowering. For the pure French stock, see Sources on page 116.

The 'Barnhavens' like a humus-rich loam or sandy soil with good drainage. Keep the roots cool and moist by mulching around the plants with shredded leaves. They prefer light, dappled shade and a high tree canopy but will take a medium-shaded, well-ventilated location without an appreciable loss of flowering performance.

Pulmonaria saccharata 'Mrs. Moon'
(lungwort)

Lungwort makes a fine edging plant; here it spills its plentiful leaves over a tree branch used to define a border.

Although lungworts are not particularly showy plants, the clusters of small bell-shaped flowers have the advantage of blooming early and over a long period when little else is in bloom. Also, several cultivars have beautiful mottled leaves. Most cultivars are blue, but, Mrs. Moon starts out as a beautiful smoky pink before turning blue. There are also pure white cultivars. A mature plant is a mound of broad, fleshy, pointed leaves 18 inches (45cm) high. It looks good as an edging along woodland paths with primroses, Lenten roses, daffodils, and other early-flowering plants. Cultivars with variegated leaves look sensational planted among hostas and ferns.

These hardy perennial plants prefer a humus-rich loam or sandy soil with reasonably good drainage. They flower best in light shade but will also flower in medium to deep shade. Plants die down in winter. They are easily propagated by division after flowering.

Rhododendron hybrids
(azaleas and rhododendrons)

Azaleas and rhododendrons are both part of the same genus, collectively known as *Rhododendron*. Azaleas tend to have small leaves and masses of small flowers that can completely hide the foliage, whereas rhododendrons usually have large, smooth, oval evergreen leaves and rounded flower clusters. At Cedaridge Farm we have some beautiful displays of aza-

Above: In areas where plants are not susceptible to mildew, 'Exbury' azaleas make magnificent shrubs for lightly shaded woodlands. Below: Spanish bluebells can literally carpet a woodland garden, here adding a splash of color to a planting that includes ferns and hostas.

leas. Though we do have a few rhododendrons, it is a struggle to get them through some of our dry summers. Azaleas certainly are much easier to grow and more widely adaptable since there are varieties, such as the southern azalea (*R. indica*), that thrive even in the Gulf states and southern California, where rhododendrons struggle in the heat.

At Cedaridge Farm we use mostly evergreen azaleas in red, pink, orange, lavender, and white (particularly the 'Kurume' hybrids), since they are the most disease-resistant. I greatly admire deciduous azaleas, such as the fragrant 'Exbury' strain (especially the yellow and orange colors), but they are prone to mildew and premature leaf drop and thus spend half the year looking like dead sticks. Without doubt, azaleas are the best flowering shrubs for light to medium shade, and a garden's reputation can be made on a good azalea display.

Azaleas like a humus-rich, fertile loam or sandy soil with excellent drainage. A gently shaded hillside is the perfect spot for them. In their natural state, they have a billowing, shrubby habit up to 8 feet (2.4m) high, or they can be sheared soon after flowering to maintain a compact cushion shape. Propagate by tip cuttings.

Scilla hispanica

(Spanish bluebells)

The botanical world doesn't seem to know what the correct botanical name is for this hardy spring-flowering bulb. It is variously listed as *Scilla, Endymion,* and *Hyacinthoides.* There are actually several types of bluebells popular in shady gardens, including the English bluebell (*S. nonscriptus*). It has the advantage of fragrance (which the Spanish bluebell does not), but it is not as easy to grow or as showy. Spanish bluebells have bell-shaped florets arranged in a spike held above the foliage. They are mostly blue, but pink and white forms are also available. At Cedaridge Farm we mass Spanish bluebells under the spreading branches of pink azaleas with primroses, ostrich ferns, and hostas for a wonderful partnership. Plants grow to 18 inches (45cm) high, produce straplike leaves, and reseed readily to create large colonies, especially on gentle slopes.

When planting the white, oval-shaped bulbs, space them at least 3 inches (7.5cm) deep from the base of the bulb and 4 inches (10cm) apart. They will grow in light to medium shade and prefer a humus-rich, well-drained loam or sandy soil. Propagate by division of the bulbs in late summer or autumn.

Tiarella cordifolia

(foamflower)

Foamflowers look sensational planted as a weed-suffocating groundcover.

Native to the Appalachian Mountains, these hardy perennials in light shade add glitter to your garden, for each white, spiky flower head resembles a sparkler throwing off a shower of sparks. Flowering in early spring at the same time as tulips, plants form low rosettes of ivy-shaped leaves. Some cultivars, like 'Dark Eyes', are darkly zoned with dark chocolate brown against a bright green background. Another coveted variety is 'Tiger Stripe', a pale pink form.

Foamflowers have also been crossed with heucheras to create an appealing rosy pink interspecific hybrid, 'Bridget Bloom'. Both foamflowers and heucheras are beautiful when planted among drifts of blue and pink creeping phlox. At Cedaridge Farm it is standard practice to add fifty foamflowers every spring along our woodland walks.

Plants grow 15 inches (37.5cm) high and spread by stoloniferous roots to create large colonies that are neither aggressive nor invasive. The species *T. wherryi* is clump-forming and lacks stolons, but in every other respect it is the same. Give foamflowers light to medium shade, a humus-rich loam or sandy soil, and good drainage. Propagate by division after flowering.

Trillium chloropetalum 'Giganteum'

(w e s t e r n   t r i l l i u m)

I am tempted to devote this space to *T. grandiflorum*, the large white eastern trillium with three-petaled flowers, since it is so popular in woodland gardens. After seeing some well-grown specimens of *T. chloropetalum*, however, I have switched my allegiance. The latter has much larger flowers in a much wider color range including white, cream, pink, red, and maroon. The flowers, which have three tapering petals held erect, rest on a beautiful collar of three heart-shaped leaves. They look sensational planted as drifts along shady streams and woodland paths with Lenten roses, primroses, azaleas, camellias, and Spanish bluebells.

Plants grow to 10 inches (25cm) high and demand a fertile, humus-rich loam or sandy soil and good drainage. Most trilliums grow best in dappled shade, but *T. chloropetalum* will take a medium-to deeply shaded location. New plants are best propagated from seed started in specially prepared shady seedbeds.

A mass planting of western trillium in a rare mix of colors creates a welcome surprise along a woodland path. This carpeting effect is possible only in areas with cool summers, mild winters, and humus-rich soil.

Tulipa hybrids
(tulip hybrids)

Though tulips are associated with sunlit fields, as seen in the production fields of Holland, the flowers are longer-lasting in light shade. Indeed, few plantings look more beautiful than a clump of a dozen or more lily-flowered tulips lighting up a woodland path. The lily-flowered are my personal favorites for woodland, because they don't look as common as the familiar Darwin tulips. Their pointed petals give them a more dignified appearance, and their color range is unusually clean and clear, especially when backlit in dappled shade. In addition to pure white, bright yellow, clear pink, lavender-mauve, and crimson red, there are dramatic bicolors such as the red-and-yellow 'Queen of Sheba' and the lavender-and-white 'Marietta'.

Plants grow to 2 feet (60cm) high from bulbs planted in autumn. Flowering occurs in spring at the same time as azaleas. Give lily-flowered tulips a humus-rich, well-drained loam or sandy soil. If you pick any of the flowers for arrangement, be sure to leave at least two of the spear-shaped leaves to help replenish the bulbs for repeat bloom. Plant bulbs 4 to 6 inches (10 to 15cm) deep from the base of the bulb and 4 inches (10cm) apart.

A mixture of cottage tulips planted in dappled shade at the entrance to Cedaridge Farm. Lily-flowered tulips have a slightly more refined quality and possess clearer colors.

Vinca minor

(periwinkle)

Ahardy, evergreen groundcover, periwinkle makes an attractive low-growing carpet of lustrous, dark green leaves and blue or white star-shaped flowers that can last for several months, starting when the soil warms in early spring. Periwinkle cultivars with variegated leaves are ideal for using in plantings that rely on diverse foliage contrasts. Native to North American woodlands, plants tolerate even deep shade, though flowering may be sparse. A related species, *V. major*, has larger flowers and leaves. Native to southern woodlands, it is not quite so hardy but still suitable for sheltered areas of the North. Also, it makes an attractive, long-lived cascading plant for containers, particularly the variegated form known as 'Surrey Marble'.

Plants grow 6 to 8 inches (15 to 20cm) high but send out runners that extend several feet in a single season. Periwinkle prefers a humus-rich loam or sandy soil and good drainage. Propagate by stem cuttings. Any 4- to 6-inch (10 to 15cm) section of stem with a leaf node will have rudimentary roots that can readily take hold in potting soil and produce a new plant.

Periwinkle flowers echo the color of the sky, sparkling among evergreen foliage along a shaded path. The plants make a dense, weed-suffocating groundcover.

Viola species and hybrids

(*v i o l a*)

There are many species and hybrids of violas suitable for shady locations, plus many hybrids such as *V. × wittrockiana* (pansies). All relish a lightly shaded location, and some of the wild species flower generously even in medium to deep shade. Sweet violets *(viola odorata)*, mostly blue, are often seen in romantic paintings of Victorian ladies clutching posies and dreaming of love. At Cedaridge Farm blue sweet violets thrive even in boggy areas, and we like to grow them close to yellow English primroses for an appealing blue-and-yellow color harmony. However, by choosing the right species, it's also possible to have violets in white and yellow.

Though the wild species flower mostly in spring, new hybrids known as violas are everblooming. If they are watered during summer heat, they will provide three seasons of color. My favorites are the 'Sorbet' and 'Penny' series, both available as mixtures with almost human "whiskered" faces. Species violets are propagated from division or seed, while hybrids are best started from seed 8 weeks before outdoor planting. Use them as low-growing annuals, since they tend to exhaust themselves after one season of continuous bloom.

Related to wild violets, perky blue violas (V. cornuta) begin flowering in early spring and will provide an entire season of bloom when fed and watered during dry spells.

Gardening
Timetable

Month-by-Month

As the seasons come and go, so do maintenance tasks in

the garden. The following garden maintenance timetables

are broken down month by month and zone by zone.

First, pinpoint your hardiness zone on the map on

page 142, and then turn to your zone in the timetable

for invaluable hands-on gardening help and information.

Whatever the season, there are planning or maintenance tasks you can do to make your
garden healthier and more beautiful.

JANUARY

1	2	3	4	5	6	7
8	9	10	11	12	13	14
15	16	17	18	19	20	21
22	23	24	25	26	27	28
29	30	31				

Zone 1

- Check winter mulch and replace if needed
- Press heaved plants back into the soil
- Study mail-order catalogs
- Order seeds, bulbs, and plants for spring
- Spray broad-leaved evergreens with antidesiccant
- Remove snow and ice from evergreens

Zone 2

- Check winter mulch and replace if needed
- Press heaved plants back into the soil
- Study mail-order catalogs
- Order seeds, bulbs, and plants for spring
- Spray broad-leaved evergreens with antidesiccant
- Remove snow and ice from evergreens

Zone 3

- Check winter mulch and replace if needed
- Press heaved plants back into the soil
- Study mail-order catalogs
- Order seeds, bulbs, and plants for spring
- Spray broad-leaved evergreens with antidesiccant
- Remove snow and ice from evergreens

Zone 4

- Check winter mulch and replace if needed
- Press heaved plants back into the soil
- Study mail-order catalogs
- Order seeds, bulbs, and plants for spring
- Spray broad-leaved evergreens with antidesiccant
- Remove snow and ice from evergreens

Zone 5

- Check winter mulch and replace if needed
- Press heaved plants back into the soil
- Study mail-order catalogs
- Order seeds, bulbs, and plants for spring
- Sow hardy and half-hardy annual seeds indoors
- Sow seeds of tender annuals that require 12 weeks or more indoors
- Spray broad-leaved evergreens with antidesiccant
- Remove snow and ice from evergreens

Zone 6

- Check winter mulch and replace if needed
- Press heaved plants back into the soil
- Study mail-order catalogs
- Order seeds, bulbs, and plants for spring
- Sow hardy and half-hardy annual seeds indoors
- Sow seeds of tender annuals that require 12 weeks or more indoors
- Spray broad-leaved evergreens with antidesiccant
- Remove snow and ice from evergreens

Zone 7

- Check winter mulch and replace if needed
- Press heaved plants back into the soil
- Study mail-order catalogs
- Order seeds, bulbs, and plants for spring
- Sow hardy and half-hardy annual seeds indoors
- Sow seeds of tender annuals that require 12 weeks or more indoors
- Spray broad-leaved evergreens with antidesiccant
- Remove snow and ice from evergreens

Zone 8

- Check winter mulch and replace if needed
- Press heaved plants back into the soil
- Study mail-order catalogs
- Order seeds, bulbs, and plants for spring
- Sow perennial and biennial seeds indoors
- Sow seeds of tender annuals that require 8 to 10 weeks indoors
- Sow seeds of hardy and half-hardy annuals indoors
- Spray broad-leaved evergreens with antidesiccant
- Remove snow and ice from evergreens

Zone 9

- Study mail-order catalogs
- Order seeds, bulbs, and plants for spring
- Plan and design the garden
- Apply mulch if frost is forecast
- Press heaved plants back into the soil
- Prepare soil for spring planting
- Test soil pH; adjust if necessary
- Plant refrigerated bulbs outdoors

- Sow annual, biennial, and perennial seeds indoors or outdoors
- Plant potted or bare-root shrubs, trees, perennials, vines, groundcovers, and B&B shrubs, trees, vines, and groundcovers
- Transplant hardy and half-hardy seedlings outdoors
- Train and prune vines
- Prune groundcovers, shade trees, and summer- and autumn-flowering shrubs and trees
- Fertilize shrubs, trees, groundcovers, vines, and perennials as growth starts
- Water if needed
- Spray dormant shrubs and trees with horticultural oil
- Divide and transplant summer- and autumn-blooming perennials
- Transplant shrubs, trees, groundcovers, and vines
- Thin overcrowded perennials and groundcovers

Zone 10

- Study mail-order catalogs
- Order seeds, bulbs, and plants for spring
- Plan and design the garden
- Prepare soil for spring planting
- Test soil pH; adjust if necessary
- Plant refrigerated bulbs outdoors
- Plant tender bulbs
- Fertilize early-flowering bulbs
- Spray with insecticides and fungicides if needed
- Spray dormant shrubs and trees with horticultural oil
- Sow annual, biennial, and perennial seeds indoors or outdoors
- Plant potted or bare-root shrubs, trees, groundcovers, vines, and flowering perennials, and B&B shrubs, trees, vines, and groundcovers

- Transplant seedlings outdoors
- Prune shade trees, ground-covers, and summer- and autumn-flowering shrubs and trees
- Train and prune vines
- Fertilize shrubs, trees, ground-covers, vines, and perennials as growth starts
- Water if needed
- Divide and transplant summer- and autumn-blooming perennials
- Transplant shrubs, trees, groundcovers, and vines
- Thin overcrowded perennials and groundcovers
- Keep the garden free of weeds

Zone 11

- Study mail-order catalogs
- Order seeds, bulbs, and plants for spring
- Plan and design the garden
- Prepare soil for spring planting
- Test soil pH; adjust if necessary
- Plant refrigerated bulbs outdoors
- Plant tender bulbs
- Fertilize early-flowering bulbs
- Spray with insecticides and fungicides if needed
- Spray dormant shrubs and trees with horticultural oil
- Sow annual, biennial, and perennial seeds indoors or outdoors
- Plant potted or bare-root shrubs, trees, groundcovers, vines, herbs, and perennials, and B&B shrubs, trees, ground-covers, and vines
- Transplant seedlings outdoors
- Prune groundcovers, shade trees, and summer- and autumn-flowering shrubs and trees
- Train and prune vines
- Fertilize shrubs, trees, ground-covers, vines, and perennials as growth starts

- Water if needed
- Divide and transplant summer- and autumn-blooming perennials
- Transplant shrubs, trees, groundcovers, and vines
- Thin overcrowded perennials and groundcovers
- Keep the garden free of weeds

FEBRUARY						
1	2	3	4	5	6	7
8	9	10	11	12	13	14
15	16	17	18	19	20	21
22	23	24	25	26	27	28

Zone 1

- Check winter mulch and add more if needed
- Press heaved plants back into the soil
- Study mail-order catalogs
- Order bulbs, seeds, and plants for spring
- Sow tender annual seeds that require 12 weeks or more indoors
- Plan and design the garden
- Prune shade trees
- Remove snow and ice from evergreens

Zone 2

- Check winter mulch and add more if needed
- Press heaved plants back into the soil
- Study mail-order catalogs
- Order bulbs, seeds, and plants for spring
- Sow tender annual seeds that require 12 weeks or more indoors
- Plan and design the garden
- Prune shade trees
- Remove snow and ice from evergreens

Zone 3

- Check winter mulch and add more if needed
- Press heaved plants back into the soil
- Study mail-order catalogs
- Order bulbs, seeds, and plants for spring
- Sow tender annual seeds indoors that require 12 weeks or more indoors
- Plan and design the garden
- Prune shade trees
- Remove snow and ice from evergreens

Zone 4

- Check winter mulch and add more if needed
- Press heaved plants back into the soil
- Study mail-order catalogs
- Order bulbs, seeds, and plants for spring
- Plan and design the garden
- Place chilled bulbs indoors for forcing
- Sow hardy and half-hardy annual seeds indoors
- Sow tender annual seeds that require 12 weeks or more indoors
- Prune shade trees
- Remove snow and ice from evergreens

Zone 5

- Check winter mulch and add more if needed
- Press heaved plants back into the soil
- Study mail-order catalogs
- Order bulbs, seeds, and plants for spring
- Plan and design the garden
- Sow tender annual seeds that require 8 to 12 weeks indoors
- Sow hardy and half-hardy annual seeds indoors
- Prune shade trees

- Remove snow and ice from evergreens

Zone 6

- Check winter mulch and add more if needed
- Press heaved plants back into the soil
- Study mail-order catalogs
- Order bulbs, seeds, and plants for spring
- Plan and design the garden
- Sow hardy and half-hardy annual seeds indoors
- Sow tender annual seeds that require 6 to 8 weeks indoors
- Prune shade trees
- Remove snow and ice from evergreens

Zone 7

- Check winter mulch and add more if needed
- Press heaved plants back into the soil
- Study mail-order catalogs
- Order bulbs, seeds, and plants for spring
- Plan and design the garden
- Sow hardy and half-hardy annual seeds indoors
- Sow tender annual seeds that require 6 to 8 weeks indoors
- Prune shade trees
- Remove snow and ice from evergreens

Zone 8

- Remove winter protection as growth starts
- Study mail-order catalogs
- Order bulbs, seeds, and plants for spring
- Plan and design the garden
- Fertilize early-flowering bulbs
- Prepare soil for planting
- Test soil pH; adjust if necessary
- Sow perennial and biennial seeds indoors and outdoors
- Sow tender annual seeds that require 4 to 6 weeks indoors

- Sow seeds of woody plants indoors or outdoors
- Sow hardy and half-hardy annual seeds outdoors
- Plant potted or bare-root shrubs, trees, groundcovers, vines, and perennials and biennials, and B&B shrubs, trees, groundcovers, and vines
- Transplant hardy and half-hardy seedlings outdoors
- Fertilize shrubs, trees, groundcovers, vines, and perennials as growth starts
- Transplant shrubs, trees, groundcovers, and vines
- Prune shade trees, groundcovers, and summer- and autumn-flowering shrubs and trees
- Prune and train vines
- Water if needed
- Spray with insecticides and fungicides if needed
- Apply horticultural oil to dormant shrubs and trees
- Divide and transplant groundcovers and summer- and autumn-blooming perennials
- Thin overcrowded groundcovers and perennials

Zone 9

- Study mail-order catalogs
- Order bulbs, seeds, and plants for spring
- Plant refrigerated bulbs outdoors
- Plant tender bulbs outdoors
- Prepare soil for planting
- Test soil pH; adjust if necessary
- Sow annual, perennial, and biennial seeds indoors and outdoors
- Sow seeds of woody plants indoors or outdoors
- Plant potted or bare-root shrubs, trees, groundcovers, vines, annuals, perennials, and biennials, and B&B shrubs, trees, groundcovers, and vines

- Transplant seedlings outdoors
- Protect tender plants from unexpected frosts
- Fertilize perennials as growth starts
- Transplant shrubs, trees, groundcovers, and vines
- Prune shade trees, groundcovers, and summer- and autumn-flowering shrubs and trees
- Train and prune vines
- Apply summer mulch
- Water plants if needed
- Fertilize early-flowering bulbs
- Start tubers, rhizomes, and tuberous roots indoors
- Spray with insecticides and fungicides if needed
- Divide and transplant groundcovers and summer- and autumn-blooming perennials
- Thin overcrowded groundcovers and perennials
- Take softwood cuttings of woody plants for rooting
- Layer stems and vines for propagating

Zone 10
- Study mail-order catalogs
- Order bulbs, seeds, and plants for spring
- Plant refrigerated bulbs outdoors
- Plant tender bulbs outdoors
- Water plants if needed
- Fertilize early-flowering bulbs
- Start tubers, rhizomes, and tuberous roots indoors
- Prepare soil for planting
- Test soil pH; adjust if necessary
- Sow annual, perennial, and biennial seeds indoors and outdoors
- Sow seeds of woody plants indoors or outdoors

- Plant potted or bare-root shrubs, trees, groundcovers, vines, annuals, perennials, and biennials, and B&B shrubs, trees, groundcovers, and vines
- Transplant seedlings outdoors
- Fertilize perennials as growth starts
- Transplant shrubs, trees, groundcovers, and vines
- Prune shade trees, groundcovers, and summer- and autumn-flowering shrubs and trees
- Train and prune vines
- Apply summer mulch
- Spray with insecticides and fungicides if needed
- Divide and transplant groundcovers and summer- and autumn-blooming perennials
- Thin overcrowded groundcovers and perennials; thin seedlings
- Take softwood cuttings of woody plants for rooting
- Layer stems and vines for propagating

Zone 11
- Study mail-order catalogs
- Order bulbs, seeds, and plants for spring
- Plant refrigerated bulbs outdoors
- Plant tender bulbs outdoors
- Water plants if needed
- Fertilize early-flowering bulbs
- Start tubers, rhizomes, and tuberous roots indoors
- Prepare soil for planting
- Test soil pH; adjust if needed
- Sow annual, perennial, and biennial seeds indoors and outdoors
- Sow seeds of woody plants indoors or outdoors

- Plant potted or bare-root shrubs, trees, groundcovers, vines, annuals, perennials, and biennials, and B&B shrubs, trees, groundcovers, and vines
- Transplant seedlings outdoors
- Fertilize perennials as growth starts
- Transplant shrubs, trees, groundcovers, and vines
- Apply summer mulch
- Prune shade trees, groundcovers, and summer- and autumn-flowering shrubs and trees
- Train and prune vines
- Spray with insecticides and fungicides if needed
- Divide and transplant groundcovers and summer- and autumn-flowering perennials
- Thin overcrowded perennials and groundcovers; thin seedlings
- Take softwood cuttings of woody plants for rooting
- Layer stems and vines for propagating

MARCH						
1	2	3	4	5	6	7
8	9	10	11	12	13	14
15	16	17	18	19	20	21
22	23	24	25	26	27	28
29	30	31				

Zone 1
- Start tubers, tuberous roots, and rhizomes indoors
- Check winter mulch; add more if needed
- Press heaved plants back into the soil
- Sow hardy and half-hardy annual, biennial, and perennial seeds indoors

- Sow tender annual seeds that require 12 weeks or more indoors
- Sow seeds of woody plants indoors
- Prune shade trees

Zone 2

- Start tubers, tuberous roots, and rhizomes indoors
- Check winter mulch; add more if needed
- Press heaved plants back into the soil
- Sow hardy and half-hardy annual, biennial, and perennial seeds indoors
- Sow tender annual seeds that require 12 weeks or more indoors
- Sow seeds of woody plants indoors
- Prune shade trees

Zone 3

- Start tubers, tuberous roots, and rhizomes indoors
- Check winter mulch; add more if needed
- Press heaved plants back into the soil
- Sow hardy and half-hardy annual, biennial, and perennial seeds indoors
- Sow tender annual seeds that require 6 to 12 weeks indoors
- Sow seeds of woody plants indoors
- Prune shade trees

Zone 4

- Start tubers, tuberous roots, and rhizomes indoors
- Remove winter protection as growth starts
- Fertilize early-flowering bulbs
- Press heaved plants back into the soil
- Sow hardy and half-hardy annual, biennial, and perennial seeds indoors

- Sow tender annual seeds that require 8 to 10 weeks indoors
- Sow seeds of woody plants indoors
- Prune shade trees

Zone 5

- Start tubers, tuberous roots, and rhizomes indoors
- Remove winter protection as growth starts
- Fertilize early-flowering bulbs
- Press heaved plants back into the soil
- Sow tender annual seeds that require 4 to 6 weeks indoors
- Sow seeds of woody plants indoors and outdoors
- Sow hardy and half-hardy seeds outdoors
- Plant hardy and half-hardy seedlings
- Prune shade trees

Zone 6

- Start tubers, tuberous roots, and rhizomes indoors
- Remove winter protection as growth starts
- Fertilize early-flowering bulbs
- Prepare soil for planting
- Test soil pH; adjust if needed
- Sow biennial and perennial seeds indoors
- Sow seeds of woody plants indoors and outdoors
- Sow tender annual seeds that require 4 to 6 weeks indoors
- Sow hardy and half-hardy seeds outdoors
- Plant hardy and half-hardy seedlings
- Plant potted or bare-root shrubs, trees, groundcovers, vines, perennials and biennials, and B&B shrubs, trees, groundcovers, and vines
- Transplant shrubs, trees, groundcovers, and vines
- Divide and transplant perennials

- Thin overcrowded groundcovers and perennials
- Prune shade trees
- Spray dormant trees and shrubs with horticultural oil

Zone 7

- Start tubers, tuberous roots, and rhizomes indoors
- Remove winter protection as growth starts
- Fertilize early-flowering bulbs
- Prepare soil for planting
- Test soil pH; adjust if needed
- Sow biennial and perennial seeds indoors
- Sow seeds of woody plants indoors and outdoors
- Sow tender annual seeds that require 4 to 6 weeks indoors
- Sow hardy and half-hardy seeds outdoors
- Plant hardy and half-hardy seedlings
- Plant potted or bare-root shrubs, trees, groundcovers, vines, perennials, and biennials, and B&B shrubs, trees, groundcovers, and vines
- Transplant shrubs, trees, groundcovers, and vines
- Divide and transplant perennials
- Thin overcrowded groundcovers and perennials
- Fertilize shrubs, trees, groundcovers, vines, and perennials as growth starts
- Keep the garden free of weeds
- Prune shade trees and summer- and autumn-flowering shrubs and trees
- Spray dormant shrubs and trees with horticultural oil

Zone 8

- Start tubers, tuberous roots, and rhizomes indoors
- Fertilize early-flowering bulbs
- Plant tender bulbs

- Sow biennial and perennial seeds indoors and outdoors
- Sow annual seeds outdoors
- Plant potted or bare-root shrubs, trees, groundcovers, vines, perennials, and biennials, and B&B shrubs, trees, groundcovers, and vines
- Plant seedlings outdoors
- Protect tender plants from unexpected frosts
- Divide and transplant summer- and autumn-flowering perennials
- Transplant shrubs, trees, groundcovers, and vines
- Thin overcrowded groundcovers and perennials; thin out seedlings
- Fertilize perennials as growth starts
- Fertilize shrubs, trees, groundcovers, and vines
- Keep the garden free of weeds
- Spray with insecticides and fungicides if needed
- Water if needed
- Prune groundcovers, shade trees, and summer- and autumn-flowering shrubs and trees
- Prune spring-flowering shrubs and trees after they bloom
- Prune and train vines
- Take softwood cuttings of woody plants for rooting
- Layer vines and stems for propagating
- Disbud flowering plants for larger blooms

Zone 9
- Fertilize bulbs, shrubs, and trees
- Plant refrigerated bulbs
- Plant summer-flowering bulbs
- Water as needed
- Spray with insecticides and fungicides if needed
- Sow annual, perennial, and biennial seeds outdoors

- Plant potted shrubs, trees, groundcovers, vines, annuals, biennials, and perennials, and B&B shrubs, trees, groundcovers, and vines
- Move seedlings outdoors
- Divide and transplant summer- and autumn-blooming perennials
- Transplant shrubs, trees, groundcovers, and vines
- Thin overcrowded groundcovers and perennials; thin out seedlings
- Prune shade trees, groundcovers, and summer- and autumn-flowering shrubs and trees
- Prune spring-flowering shrubs and trees after they bloom
- Prune and train vines
- Shear fine-needled evergreens as needed
- Fertilize perennials as growth starts
- Keep the garden free of weeds
- Apply summer mulch
- Stake tall plants
- Disbud flowering plants for larger blooms
- Remove faded flowers

Zone 10
- Fertilize bulbs, shrubs, and trees
- Plant refrigerated bulbs
- Plant summer-flowering bulbs
- Water as needed
- Spray with insecticides and fungicides if needed
- Sow annual, perennial, and biennial seeds outdoors
- Plant potted shrubs, trees, groundcovers, vines, annuals, biennials, and perennials, and B&B shrubs, trees, groundcovers, and vines
- Move seedlings outdoors
- Divide and transplant summer- and autumn-blooming perennials

- Transplant shrubs, trees, groundcovers, and vines
- Thin overcrowded groundcovers and perennials; thin seedlings
- Prune shade trees, groundcovers, and summer- and autumn-flowering shrubs and trees
- Prune spring-flowering shrubs and trees after they bloom
- Prune and train vines
- Shear fine-needled evergreens as needed
- Fertilize perennials as growth starts
- Keep the garden free of weeds
- Apply summer mulch
- Stake tall plants
- Disbud flowering plants for larger blooms
- Remove faded flowers

Zone 11
- Fertilize bulbs, shrubs, and trees
- Plant refrigerated bulbs
- Plant summer-flowering bulbs
- Water as needed
- Spray with insecticides and fungicides if needed
- Sow annual, perennial, and biennial seeds outdoors
- Plant potted shrubs, trees, groundcovers, vines, annuals, biennials, and perennials, and B&B shrubs, trees, groundcovers, and vines
- Move seedlings outdoors
- Divide and transplant summer- and autumn-blooming perennials
- Transplant shrubs, trees, groundcovers, and vines
- Thin overcrowded groundcovers and perennials; thin seedlings
- Prune shade trees, groundcovers, and summer- and autumn-flowering shrubs and trees

- Prune spring-flowering shrubs and trees after they bloom
- Prune and train vines
- Shear fine-needled evergreens as needed
- Fertilize perennials as growth starts
- Keep the garden free of weeds
- Apply summer mulch
- Stake tall plants
- Disbud flowering plants for larger blooms
- Remove faded flowers

APRIL

1	2	3	4	5	6	7
8	9	10	11	12	13	14
15	16	17	18	19	20	21
22	23	24	25	26	27	28
29	30					

Zone 1

- Remove winter protection as growth starts
- Fertilize early-flowering bulbs
- Start rhizomes, tubers, and tuberous roots indoors
- Prepare soil for planting
- Test soil pH; adjust if needed
- Sow perennial and biennial seeds indoors
- Sow hardy and half-hardy annual seeds indoors
- Sow tender annual seeds that require 6 to 10 weeks indoors
- Plant potted or bare-root shrubs, trees, groundcovers, vines, perennials and biennials, and B&B shrubs, trees, ground-covers, and vines
- Transplant shrubs, trees, groundcovers, and vines
- Prune groundcovers
- Train and prune vines
- Prune shade trees and summer- and autumn-flowering shrubs and trees

- Thin overcrowded perennials and groundcovers
- Fertilize shrubs, trees, ground-covers, vines, and perennials as growth starts
- Keep the garden free of weeds
- Spray dormant shrubs and trees with horticultural oil

Zone 2

- Remove winter protection as growth starts
- Fertilize early-flowering bulbs
- Start rhizomes, tubers, and tuberous roots indoors
- Prepare soil for planting
- Test soil pH; adjust if needed
- Sow perennial and biennial seeds indoors
- Sow hardy and half-hardy annual seeds indoors
- Sow tender annual seeds that require 6 to 10 weeks indoors
- Plant potted or bare-root shrubs, trees, groundcovers, vines, perennials, and biennials, and B&B shrubs, trees, ground-covers, and vines
- Transplant shrubs, trees, groundcovers, vines and perennials
- Prune groundcovers
- Prune shade trees and summer- and autumn-flowering shrubs and trees
- Train and prune vines
- Thin overcrowded perennials and groundcovers
- Fertilize shrubs, trees, ground-covers, vines, and perennials as growth starts
- Keep the garden free of weeds
- Spray dormant shrubs and trees with horticultural oil

Zone 3

- Remove winter protection as growth starts
- Fertilize early-flowering bulbs

- Start rhizomes, tubers, and tuberous roots indoors
- Prepare soil for planting
- Test soil pH; adjust if needed
- Sow perennial and biennial seeds indoors
- Sow tender annual seeds that require 4 to 6 weeks indoors
- Plant potted or bare-root shrubs, trees, groundcovers, vines, perennials, and biennials, and B&B shrubs, trees, ground-covers, and vines
- Thin overcrowded plantings of perennials and groundcovers
- Fertilize shrubs, trees, ground-covers, vines, and perennials as growth starts
- Transplant shrubs, trees, groundcovers, and vines
- Prune groundcovers
- Prune shade trees and summer- and autumn-flowering shrubs and trees
- Train and prune vines
- Keep the garden free of weeds
- Spray dormant shrubs and trees with horticultural oil

Zone 4

- Remove winter protection as growth starts
- Transplant and divide early-flowering bulbs
- Prepare soil for planting
- Test soil pH; adjust if needed
- Sow annual, perennial, and biennial seeds indoors
- Sow hardy and half-hardy annual seeds outdoors
- Plant hardy and half-hardy annual seedlings outdoors
- Plant potted or bare-root shrubs, trees, groundcovers, vines, perennials and biennials, and B&B shrubs, trees, ground-covers, and vines
- Transplant shrubs, trees, groundcovers, and vines

- Prune groundcovers
- Prune shade trees and summer- and autumn-flowering shrubs and trees
- Train and prune vines
- Thin overcrowded perennials and groundcovers
- Fertilize shrubs, trees, groundcovers, vines, and perennials as growth starts
- Keep the garden free of weeds
- Spray dormant shrubs and trees with horticultural oil

Zone 5

- Remove winter protection as growth starts
- Transplant and divide early-flowering bulbs
- Prepare soil for planting
- Test soil pH; adjust if needed
- Sow perennial, and biennial seeds indoors
- Sow hardy and half-hardy annual seeds outdoors
- Plant hardy and half-hardy seedlings outdoors
- Plant potted or bare-root shrubs, trees, groundcovers, vines, perennials and biennials, and B&B shrubs, trees, groundcovers, and vines
- Transplant shrubs, trees, groundcovers, and vines
- Protect tender plants from unexpected frosts if needed
- Prune groundcovers
- Prune shade trees and summer- and autumn-flowering shrubs and trees
- Train and prune vines
- Thin overcrowded perennials and groundcovers
- Fertilize shrubs, trees, groundcovers, vines, and perennials as growth starts
- Keep the garden free of weeds
- Spray dormant shrubs and trees with horticultural oil

Zone 6

- Remove winter protection as growth starts
- Transplant and divide early-flowering bulbs
- Fertilize early-flowering bulbs
- Prepare soil for planting
- Test soil pH; adjust if needed
- Sow perennial and biennial seeds indoors or outdoors
- Sow hardy and half-hardy annual seeds outdoors
- Move hardy and half-hardy seedlings outdoors
- Plant potted or bare-root shrubs, trees, groundcovers, vines, perennials, and biennials, and B&B shrubs, trees, groundcovers, and vines
- Transplant shrubs, trees, groundcovers, and vines
- Protect tender plants from unexpected frosts if needed
- Prune groundcovers
- Prune shade trees and summer- and autumn-flowering shrubs and trees
- Train and prune vines
- Thin overcrowded perennials, seedlings, and groundcovers
- Fertilize shrubs, trees, groundcovers, vines, and perennials as growth starts
- Keep the garden free of weeds
- Spray dormant shrubs and trees with horticultural oil

Zone 7

- Transplant and divide early-flowering bulbs
- Fertilize early-flowering bulbs
- Prepare soil for planting
- Test soil pH; adjust if needed
- Sow perennial and biennial seeds indoors and outdoors
- Sow hardy and half-hardy seeds outdoors
- Move hardy and half-hardy seedlings outdoors

- Plant potted or bare-root shrubs, trees, groundcovers, vines, perennials, and biennials, and B&B shrubs, trees, groundcovers, and vines
- Transplant shrubs, trees, groundcovers, and vines
- Protect tender plants from unexpected frosts if needed
- Prune groundcovers
- Prune shade trees and summer- and autumn-flowering shrubs and trees
- Prune spring-flowering shrubs and trees after they bloom
- Train and prune vines
- Divide and transplant perennials and groundcovers
- Thin overcrowded perennials, seedlings, and groundcovers
- Fertilize shrubs, trees, groundcovers, vines, and perennials as growth starts
- Stake tall plants
- Keep the garden free of weeds
- Spray with insecticides and fungicides if needed

Zone 8

- Transplant and divide early-flowering bulbs
- Fertilize early-flowering bulbs
- Plant summer-flowering bulbs
- Sow annual, biennial, and perennial seeds outdoors
- Plant potted shrubs, trees, groundcovers, vines, and perennials, and B&B shrubs, trees, groundcovers, and vines
- Move seedlings outdoors
- Thin seedlings
- Prune shade trees and summer- and autumn-flowering shrubs and trees
- Shear fine-needled evergreens as needed
- Prune spring-flowering shrubs and trees after they bloom
- Prune groundcovers if needed; train and prune vines

- Water as needed
- Spray with insecticides and fungicides if needed
- Keep the garden free of weeds
- Apply summer mulch
- Stake tall plants
- Fertilize plants as needed
- Remove faded flowers
- Disbud flowers for larger blooms

Zone 9

- Transplant and divide early-flowering bulbs
- Fertilize early-flowering bulbs
- Plant summer-flowering bulbs
- Plant potted shrubs, trees, groundcovers, vines, and perennials, and B&B shrubs, trees, groundcovers, and vines
- Prune shade trees and summer- and autumn-flowering shrubs and trees
- Prune spring-flowering shrubs and trees after they bloom
- Prune groundcovers if needed; train and prune vines
- Keep the garden free of weeds
- Sow annual, biennial, and perennial seeds outdoors
- Move seedlings outdoors
- Thin seedlings
- Water as needed
- Spray with insecticides and fungicides if needed
- Fertilize plants as needed
- Disbud flowering plants for larger blooms
- Remove faded flowers
- Pinch annuals and perennials as needed

Zone 10

- Transplant and divide early-flowering bulbs
- Fertilize early-flowering bulbs
- Plant summer-flowering bulbs
- Plant potted shrubs, trees, groundcovers, vines, and perennials, and B&B shrubs, trees, groundcovers, and vines

- Prune shade trees and summer- and autumn-flowering shrubs and trees
- Prune spring-flowering shrubs and trees after they bloom
- Prune groundcovers if needed; train and prune vines
- Keep the garden free of weeds
- Sow annual, biennial, and perennial seeds outdoors
- Move seedlings outdoors
- Thin seedlings
- Water as needed
- Spray with insecticides and fungicides if needed
- Fertilize plants as needed
- Disbud flowering plants for larger blooms
- Remove faded flowers
- Pinch annuals and perennials as needed

Zone 11

- Transplant and divide early-flowering bulbs
- Fertilize early-flowering bulbs
- Plant summer-flowering bulbs
- Plant potted shrubs, trees, groundcovers, vines, and perennials, and B&B shrubs, trees, groundcovers, and vines
- Prune shade trees and summer- and autumn-flowering shrubs and trees
- Prune spring-flowering shrubs and trees after they bloom
- Prune groundcovers if needed; train and prune vines
- Keep the garden free of weeds
- Sow annual, biennial, and perennial seeds outdoors
- Move seedlings outdoors
- Water as needed
- Spray with insecticides and fungicides if needed
- Fertilize plants as needed
- Disbud flowering plants for larger blooms
- Remove faded flowers
- Pinch annuals and perennials as needed

MAY						
1	2	3	4	5	6	7
8	9	10	11	12	13	14
15	16	17	18	19	20	21
22	23	24	25	26	27	28
29	30	31				

Zone 1

- Prepare soil for planting
- Fertilize early-flowering bulbs
- Divide and transplant early-flowering bulbs
- Sow perennial and biennial seeds outdoors
- Sow hardy and half-hardy annual seeds outdoors
- Sow tender annual seeds that require 4 to 6 weeks indoors
- Plant potted or bare-root shrubs, trees, groundcovers, vines, perennials, and biennials, and B&B shrubs, trees, groundcovers, and vines
- Transplant perennial, biennial, and hardy and half-hardy annual seedlings outdoors
- Transplant shrubs, trees, groundcovers, and vines
- Thin overcrowded groundcovers and perennials
- Prune shade trees and summer- and autumn-flowering shrubs and trees
- Prune groundcovers
- Train and prune vines
- Divide and transplant groundcovers and perennials
- Fertilize shrubs, trees, groundcovers, vines, and perennials as growth starts
- Keep the garden free of weeds
- Spray with insecticides and fungicides if needed
- Water as needed
- Take stem cuttings of woody plants for rooting
- Layer stems and vines for propagating

- Disbud flowering plants for larger blooms
- Apply summer mulch

Zone 2

- Prepare soil for planting
- Fertilize early-flowering bulbs
- Divide and transplant early-flowering bulbs
- Sow perennial and biennial seeds outdoors
- Sow seeds of hardy and half-hardy annuals outdoors
- Sow tender annual seeds that require 4 to 6 weeks indoors
- Plant potted or bare-root shrubs, trees, groundcovers, vines, perennials and biennials, and B&B shrubs, trees, groundcovers, and vines
- Transplant perennial, biennial, and hardy and half-hardy annual and vegetable seedlings outdoors
- Transplant shrubs, trees, groundcovers, and vines
- Prune shade trees and summer- and autumn-flowering shrubs and trees
- Prune groundcovers
- Train and prune vines
- Thin overcrowded groundcovers and perennials
- Divide and transplant groundcovers and perennials
- Fertilize shrubs, trees, groundcovers, vines, and perennials as growth starts
- Keep the garden free of weeds
- Spray with insecticides and fungicides if needed
- Water as needed
- Take stem cuttings of woody plants for rooting
- Layer stems and vines for propagating
- Disbud flowering plants for larger blooms
- Apply summer mulch
- Sow grass seed

Zone 3

- Prepare soil for planting
- Fertilize early-flowering bulbs
- Divide and transplant early-flowering bulbs
- Plant summer-flowering bulbs
- Sow perennial and biennial seeds outdoors
- Sow hardy and half-hardy annual seeds outdoors
- Sow tender annual seeds that require 4 to 6 weeks indoors
- Plant potted or bare-root shrubs, trees, groundcovers, vines, perennials, and biennials, and B&B shrubs, trees, groundcovers, and vines
- Transplant perennial, biennial, and hardy and half-hardy annual seedlings outdoors
- Transplant shrubs, trees, groundcovers, and vines
- Protect tender plants from unexpected frosts if needed
- Prune shade trees and summer- and autumn-flowering shrubs and trees
- Prune groundcovers
- Train and prune vines
- Thin overcrowded perennials and groundcovers
- Divide and transplant groundcovers and perennials
- Fertilize shrubs, trees, groundcovers, vines, and perennials as growth starts
- Keep the garden free of weeds
- Spray with insecticides and fungicides if needed
- Water as needed
- Take stem cuttings of woody plants for rooting
- Layer stems and vines for propagating
- Disbud flowering plants for larger blooms
- Apply summer mulch

Zone 4

- Divide and transplant spring-flowering bulbs
- Fertilize bulbs
- Plant summer-flowering bulbs
- Sow perennial and biennial seeds outdoors
- Sow hardy and half-hardy annual seeds outdoors
- Plant potted or bare-root shrubs, trees, groundcovers, vines, perennials, and biennials, and B&B shrubs, trees, groundcovers, and vines
- Transplant perennial, biennial, and hardy and half-hardy annual seedlings outdoors
- Transplant shrubs, trees, groundcovers, and vines
- Protect tender plants from unexpected frosts if needed
- Prune shade trees and summer- and autumn-flowering shrubs and trees
- Prune groundcovers
- Train and prune vines
- Thin overcrowded perennials, seedlings, and groundcovers
- Divide and transplant groundcovers and perennials
- Fertilize shrubs, trees, groundcovers, vines, and perennials as growth starts
- Keep the garden free of weeds
- Spray with insecticides and fungicides if needed
- Water as needed
- Take stem cuttings of woody plants for rooting
- Layer stems and vines for propagating
- Disbud flowering plants for larger blooms
- Apply summer mulch

Zone 5

- Divide and transplant spring-flowering bulbs
- Fertilize bulbs

- Plant summer-flowering bulbs
- Remove faded flowers
- Remove dead bulb foliage
- Sow annual, perennial, and biennial seeds outdoors
- Move seedlings outdoors
- Thin overgrown perennials, seedlings, and groundcovers
- Plant potted shrubs, trees, groundcovers, vines, and perennials, and B&B shrubs, trees, groundcovers, and vines
- Divide and transplant groundcovers and perennials
- Fertilize groundcovers and perennials as growth starts
- Prune shade trees and summer- and autumn-flowering shrubs and trees
- Prune spring-flowering shrubs and trees after they bloom
- Shear fine-needled evergreens as needed
- Prune groundcovers
- Train and prune vines
- Keep the garden free of weeds
- Water as needed
- Spray with insecticides and fungicides if needed
- Disbud flowering plants for larger blooms
- Apply summer mulch
- Take stem cuttings of woody plants for rooting
- Layer stems and vines for propagating

Zone 6

- Divide and transplant spring-flowering bulbs
- Fertilize bulbs
- Plant summer-flowering bulbs
- Remove faded flowers
- Remove dead bulb foliage
- Sow annual, perennial, and biennial seeds outdoors
- Move seedlings outdoors
- Thin overgrown perennials, seedlings, and groundcovers

- Plant potted shrubs, trees, groundcovers, vines, and perennials, and B&B shrubs, trees, groundcovers, and vines
- Prune shade trees and summer- and autumn-flowering shrubs and trees
- Prune spring-flowering shrubs and trees after they bloom
- Prune groundcovers
- Train and prune vines
- Shear fine-needled evergreens as needed
- Divide and transplant groundcovers and perennials
- Fertilize groundcovers and perennials as growth starts
- Keep the garden free of weeds
- Water as needed
- Spray with insecticides and fungicides if needed
- Disbud flowering plants for larger blooms
- Apply summer mulch
- Take stem cuttings of woody plants for rooting
- Layer stems and vines for propagating

Zone 7

- Divide and transplant spring-flowering bulbs
- Fertilize bulbs
- Plant summer-flowering bulbs
- Remove faded flowers
- Remove dead bulb foliage
- Sow annual, perennial, and biennial seeds outdoors
- Move seedlings outdoors
- Thin overgrown groundcovers, seedlings, and perennials
- Plant potted shrubs, trees, groundcovers, vines, and perennials, and B&B shrubs, trees, groundcovers, and vines
- Divide and transplant groundcovers and perennials
- Fertilize groundcovers and perennials as growth starts

- Prune shade trees and summer- and autumn-flowering shrubs and trees
- Prune spring-flowering shrubs and trees after they bloom
- Shear fine-needled evergreens as needed
- Prune groundcovers
- Train and prune vines
- Keep the garden free of weeds
- Water as needed
- Spray with insecticides and fungicides if needed
- Disbud flowering plants for larger blooms
- Apply summer mulch
- Take stem cuttings of woody plants for rooting
- Layer stems and vines for propagating

Zone 8

- Divide and transplant spring-flowering bulbs
- Continue to plant summer-flowering bulbs
- Remove faded flowers
- Remove dead bulb foliage
- Plant potted shrubs, trees, groundcovers, vines, and perennials, and B&B shrubs, trees, groundcovers, and vines
- Move seedlings outdoors
- Fertilize plants as needed
- Prune shade trees
- Prune groundcovers
- Train and prune vines
- Keep the garden free of weeds
- Water as needed
- Spray with insecticides and fungicides if needed
- Apply summer mulch
- Pinch annuals and perennials as needed
- Disbud flowering plants for larger blooms
- Take stem cuttings of woody plants for rooting
- Layer stems and vines for propagating

Zone 9

- Divide and transplant spring-flowering bulbs
- Continue to plant summer-flowering bulbs
- Remove faded flowers
- Remove dead bulb foliage
- Plant potted shrubs, trees, groundcovers, vines, and perennials, and B&B shrubs, trees, groundcovers, and vines
- Add summer annuals to the garden
- Sow seeds outdoors for succession plantings
- Prune shade trees
- Prune groundcovers; shear low-growing plants
- Train and prune vines
- Fertilize plants as needed
- Keep the garden free of weeds
- Water as needed
- Spray with insecticides and fungicides if needed
- Apply summer mulch
- Pinch annuals and perennials as needed
- Disbud flowering plants for larger blooms
- Take stem cuttings of woody plants for rooting
- Layer stems and vines for propagating

Zone 10

- Divide and transplant spring-flowering bulbs
- Continue to plant summer-flowering bulbs
- Remove faded flowers
- Remove dead bulb foliage
- Plant potted shrubs, trees, groundcovers, vines, and perennials, and B&B shrubs, trees, groundcovers, and vines
- Add summer annuals to the garden
- Prune shade trees

- Prune groundcovers; shear low-growing plants
- Train and prune vines
- Fertilize plants as needed
- Keep the garden free of weeds
- Water as needed
- Spray with insecticides and fungicides if needed
- Apply summer mulch
- Pinch annuals and perennials as needed
- Disbud flowering plants for larger blooms
- Take stem cuttings of woody plants for rooting
- Layer stems and vines for propagating

Zone 11

- Divide and transplant spring-flowering bulbs
- Continue to plant summer-flowering bulbs
- Remove faded flowers
- Remove dead bulb foliage
- Plant potted shrubs, trees, groundcovers, vines, and perennials, and B&B shrubs, trees, groundcovers, and vines
- Add summer annuals to the garden
- Prune shade trees
- Prune groundcovers; shear low-growing plants
- Train and prune vines
- Fertilize plants as needed
- Keep the garden free of weeds
- Water as needed
- Spray with insecticides and fungicides if needed
- Apply summer mulch
- Pinch annuals and perennials as needed
- Disbud flowering plants for larger blooms
- Take stem cuttings of woody plants for rooting
- Layer stems and vines for propagating

JUNE						
1	2	3	4	5	6	7
8	9	10	11	12	13	14
15	16	17	18	19	20	21
22	23	24	25	26	27	28
29	30					

Zone 1

- Plant summer-flowering bulbs
- Remove dead bulb foliage
- Fertilize bulbs; fertilize other plants as needed
- Remove faded flowers
- Plant potted shrubs, trees, groundcovers, vines, and perennials, and B&B shrubs, trees, groundcovers, and vines
- Prune groundcovers as needed
- Train and prune vines as needed
- Sow annual, biennial, and perennial seeds outdoors
- Move seedlings outdoors
- Thin seedlings
- Protect tender plants from unexpected frosts if needed
- Prune spring-flowering shrubs after they bloom
- Shear fine-needled evergreens and formal hedges
- Water as needed
- Apply summer mulch
- Spray with insecticides and fungicides if needed
- Disbud flowering plants for larger blooms

Zone 2

- Plant summer-flowering bulbs
- Remove dead bulb foliage
- Fertilize bulbs; fertilize other plants as needed
- Remove faded flowers
- Plant potted shrubs, trees, groundcovers, vines, and perennials, and B&B shrubs, trees, groundcovers, and vines

- Prune groundcovers as needed
- Train and prune vines as needed
- Sow annual, biennial, and perennial seeds outdoors
- Move seedlings outdoors
- Thin seedlings
- Protect tender plants from unexpected frosts if needed
- Prune spring-flowering shrubs after they bloom
- Shear fine-needled evergreens and formal hedges
- Stake tall plants
- Keep the garden free of weeds
- Water if needed
- Apply summer mulch
- Spray with insecticides and fungicides if needed
- Disbud flowering plants for larger blooms

Zone 3

- Plant summer-flowering bulbs
- Remove dead bulb foliage
- Fertilize bulbs; fertilize other plants as needed
- Remove faded flowers
- Plant potted shrubs, trees, groundcovers, vines, and perennials, and B&B shrubs, trees, groundcovers, and vines
- Prune groundcovers as needed
- Train and prune vines as needed
- Sow annual, biennial, and perennial seeds outdoors
- Move seedlings outdoors
- Thin seedlings
- Prune spring-flowering shrubs after they bloom
- Shear fine-needled evergreens and formal hedges
- Stake tall plants
- Keep the garden free of weeds
- Water as needed
- Apply summer mulch
- Spray with insecticides and fungicides if needed
- Disbud flowering plants for larger blooms

Zone 4

- Remove dead bulb foliage
- Fertilize bulbs; fertilize other plants as needed
- Remove faded flowers
- Plant potted shrubs, trees, groundcovers, vines, and perennials, and B&B shrubs, trees, groundcovers, and vines
- Prune groundcovers as needed
- Train and prune vines as needed
- Sow annual, biennial, and perennial seeds outdoors
- Move seedlings outdoors
- Thin seedlings
- Prune spring-flowering shrubs after they bloom
- Shear fine-needled evergreens and formal hedges
- Stake tall plants
- Keep the garden free of weeds
- Water as needed
- Apply summer mulch
- Spray with insecticides and fungicides if needed
- Disbud flowering plants for larger blooms

Zone 5

- Remove dead bulb foliage
- Fertilize bulbs; fertilize other plants as needed
- Remove faded flowers
- Plant potted shrubs, trees, groundcovers, vines, and perennials, and B&B shrubs, trees, groundcovers, and vines
- Prune groundcovers as needed
- Thin seedlings
- Train and prune vines as needed
- Prune spring-flowering shrubs after they bloom
- Shear formal hedges
- Keep the garden free of weeds
- Stake tall plants
- Water as needed
- Apply summer mulch
- Spray with insecticides and fungicides if needed

- Pinch annuals and perennials as needed
- Disbud flowering plants for larger blooms

Zone 6

- Remove dead bulb foliage
- Fertilize bulbs; fertilize other plants as needed
- Remove faded flowers
- Plant potted shrubs, trees, groundcovers, vines, and perennials, and B&B shrubs, trees, groundcovers, and vines
- Prune groundcovers as needed
- Train and prune vines as needed
- Thin seedlings
- Prune spring-flowering shrubs after they bloom
- Shear formal hedges
- Keep the garden free of weeds
- Stake tall plants
- Water as needed
- Apply summer mulch
- Spray with insecticides and fungicides if needed
- Pinch annuals and perennials as needed
- Disbud flowering plants for larger blooms

Zone 7

- Remove dead bulb foliage
- Fertilize bulbs; fertilize other plants as needed
- Remove faded flowers
- Plant potted shrubs, trees, groundcovers, vines, and perennials, and B&B shrubs, trees, groundcovers, and vines
- Prune groundcovers as needed
- Train and prune vines as needed
- Prune spring-flowering shrubs after they bloom
- Thin seedlings
- Shear formal hedges
- Keep the garden free of weeds
- Stake tall plants
- Water as needed

- Apply summer mulch
- Spray with insecticides and fungicides if needed
- Pinch annuals and perennials as needed
- Disbud flowering plants for larger blooms

Zone 8

- Remove dead bulb foliage
- Fertilize bulbs; fertilize other plants as needed
- Remove faded flowers
- Plant potted shrubs, trees, groundcovers, vines, and perennials, and B&B shrubs, trees, groundcovers, and vines
- Sow seeds outdoors for succession plantings
- Prune groundcovers as needed; shear low-growing plants
- Train and prune vines as needed
- Shear formal hedges
- Keep the garden free of weeds
- Water as needed
- Spray with insecticides and fungicides if needed
- Pinch annuals and perennials as needed
- Disbud flowering plants for larger blooms

Zone 9

- Remove dead bulb foliage
- Fertilize bulbs; fertilize other plants as needed
- Remove faded flowers
- Plant potted shrubs, trees, groundcovers, vines, and perennials, and B&B shrubs, trees, groundcovers, and vines
- Prune groundcovers as needed; shear low-growing plants
- Train and prune vines as needed
- Shear formal hedges
- Keep the garden free of weeds
- Water as needed
- Spray with insecticides and fungicides if needed

- Pinch annuals and perennials as needed
- Disbud flowering plants for larger blooms
- Remove hardy and half-hardy annuals as they fade

Zone 10

- Remove dead bulb foliage
- Fertilize bulbs; fertilize other plants as needed
- Remove faded flowers
- Plant potted shrubs, trees, groundcovers, vines, and perennials, and B&B shrubs, trees, groundcovers, and vines
- Prune groundcovers as needed; shear low-growing plants
- Train and prune vines as needed
- Shear formal hedges
- Keep the garden free of weeds
- Water as needed
- Spray with insecticides and fungicides if needed
- Pinch annuals and perennials as needed
- Disbud flowering plants for larger blooms
- Remove hardy and half-hardy annuals as they fade

Zone 11

- Remove dead bulb foliage
- Fertilize bulbs; fertilize other plants as needed
- Remove faded flowers
- Plant potted shrubs, trees, groundcovers, vines, and perennials, and B&B shrubs, trees, groundcovers, and vines
- Prune groundcovers as needed; shear low-growing plants
- Train and prune vines as needed
- Shear formal hedges
- Keep the garden free of weeds
- Water as needed
- Spray with insecticides and fungicides if needed
- Pinch annuals and perennials as needed

- Disbud flowering plants for larger blooms
- Remove hardy and half-hardy annuals as they fade

JULY						
1	2	3	4	5	6	7
8	9	10	11	12	13	14
15	16	17	18	19	20	21
22	23	24	25	26	27	28
29	30	31				

Zone 1

- Order spring-flowering bulbs
- Plant potted shrubs, trees, groundcovers, perennials, and biennials, and B&B shrubs, trees, groundcovers, and vines
- Sow perennial and biennial seeds outdoors
- Fertilize plants as needed
- Keep the garden free of weeds
- Remove faded flowers
- Shear low-growing plants
- Pinch annuals and perennials until midmonth
- Prune groundcovers; trim edges
- Train and prune vines as needed
- Disbud flowering plants for larger blooms
- Stake tall plants
- Water as needed
- Spray with insecticides and fungicides if needed
- Take softwood cuttings for rooting

Zone 2

- Order spring-flowering bulbs
- Plant potted shrubs, trees, groundcovers, vines, perennials, and biennials, and B&B shrubs, trees, groundcovers, and vines
- Sow perennial and biennial seeds outdoors
- Fertilize plants as needed
- Keep the garden free of weeds

- Remove faded flowers
- Shear low-growing plants
- Pinch annuals and perennials until midmonth
- Prune groundcovers; trim edges
- Train and prune vines as needed
- Disbud flowering plants for larger blooms
- Stake tall plants
- Water as needed
- Spray with insecticides and fungicides if needed
- Take softwood cuttings for rooting

Zone 3
- Order spring-flowering bulbs
- Plant potted shrubs, trees, groundcovers, vines, perennials, and biennials, and B&B shrubs, trees, groundcovers, and vines
- Sow perennial and biennial seeds outdoors
- Fertilize plants as needed
- Keep the garden free of weeds
- Remove faded flowers
- Shear low-growing plants
- Pinch annuals and perennials until midmonth
- Prune groundcovers; trim edges
- Train and prune vines as needed
- Disbud flowering plants for larger blooms
- Stake tall plants
- Water as needed
- Spray with insecticides and fungicides if needed
- Take softwood cuttings for rooting

Zone 4
- Order spring-flowering bulbs
- Plant potted shrubs, trees, groundcovers, vines, perennials, and biennials, and B&B shrubs, trees, groundcovers, and vines
- Sow perennial and biennial seeds outdoors
- Fertilize plants as needed
- Keep the garden free of weeds

- Remove faded flowers
- Shear low-growing plants
- Pinch annuals and perennials until midmonth
- Prune groundcovers; trim edges
- Train and prune vines as needed
- Disbud flowering plants for larger blooms
- Stake tall plants
- Water as needed
- Spray with insecticides and fungicides if needed
- Take softwood cuttings for rooting

Zone 5
- Order spring-flowering bulbs
- Plant potted shrubs, trees, groundcovers, vines, perennials, and biennials, and B&B shrubs, trees, groundcovers, and vines
- Sow perennial and biennial seeds outdoors
- Keep the garden free of weeds
- Fertilize plants as needed
- Remove faded flowers
- Shear low-growing plants
- Pinch annuals and perennials until midmonth
- Prune groundcovers; trim edges
- Train and prune vines as needed
- Disbud flowering plants for larger blooms
- Stake tall plants
- Water as needed
- Spray with insecticides and fungicides if needed
- Take softwood cuttings for rooting

Zone 6
- Order spring-flowering bulbs
- Plant potted shrubs, trees, groundcovers, vines, perennials, and biennials, and B&B shrubs, trees, groundcovers, and vines
- Sow perennial and biennial seeds outdoors
- Keep the garden free of weeds
- Fertilize plants as needed

- Remove faded flowers
- Shear low-growing plants
- Pinch annuals and perennials until midmonth
- Prune groundcovers; trim edges
- Train and prune vines as needed
- Disbud flowering plants for larger blooms
- Stake tall plants
- Water as needed
- Spray with insecticides and fungicides if needed
- Take softwood cuttings for rooting

Zone 7
- Order spring-flowering bulbs
- Plant potted shrubs, trees, groundcovers, vines, perennials, and biennials, and B&B shrubs, trees, groundcovers, and vines
- Sow perennial and biennial seeds outdoors
- Sow seeds for succession plantings
- Keep the garden free of weeds
- Fertilize plants as needed
- Remove faded flowers
- Shear low-growing plants
- Pinch annuals and perennials until midmonth
- Prune groundcovers; trim edges
- Train and prune vines as needed
- Disbud flowering plants for larger blooms
- Stake tall plants
- Water as needed
- Spray with insecticides and fungicides if needed
- Take softwood cuttings for rooting

Zone 8
- Order spring-flowering bulbs
- Plant potted shrubs, trees, groundcovers, vines, perennials, and biennials, and B&B shrubs, trees, groundcovers, and vines
- Keep the garden free of weeds
- Fertilize as needed

- Remove faded flowers
- Pinch annuals and perennials until midmonth
- Prune groundcovers; trim edges
- Train and prune vines as needed
- Disbud flowering plants for larger blooms
- Shear low-growing plants
- Stake tall plants
- Water as needed
- Spray with insecticides and fungicides if needed
- Take softwood cuttings for rooting

Zone 9
- Order spring-flowering bulbs
- Plant potted shrubs, trees, groundcovers, vines, perennials, and biennials, and B&B shrubs, trees, groundcovers, and vines
- Keep the garden free of weeds
- Fertilize plants as needed
- Remove faded flowers
- Pinch annuals and perennials as needed
- Prune groundcovers; trim edges
- Train and prune vines as needed
- Disbud flowering plants for larger blooms
- Shear low-growing plants
- Stake tall plants
- Water as needed
- Spray with insecticides and fungicides if needed
- Take softwood cuttings for rooting

Zone 10
- Order spring-flowering bulbs
- Plant potted shrubs, trees, groundcovers, vines, perennials, and biennials, and B&B shrubs, trees, groundcovers, and vines
- Keep the garden free of weeds
- Fertilize plants as needed
- Remove faded flowers
- Pinch annuals and perennials as needed
- Prune groundcovers; trim edges

- Train and prune vines as needed
- Disbud flowering plants for larger blooms
- Shear low-growing plants
- Stake tall plants
- Water as needed
- Spray with insecticides and fungicides if needed
- Take softwood cuttings for rooting

Zone 11
- Order spring-flowering bulbs
- Plant potted shrubs, trees, groundcovers, vines, perennials, and biennials, and B&B shrubs, trees, groundcovers, and vines
- Keep the garden free of weeds
- Fertilize plants as needed
- Remove faded flowers
- Pinch annuals and perennials as needed
- Prune groundcovers; trim edges
- Train and prune vines as needed
- Disbud flowering plants for larger blooms
- Shear low-growing plants
- Stake tall plants
- Water as needed
- Spray with insecticides and fungicides if needed
- Take softwood cuttings for rooting

AUGUST						
1	2	3	4	5	6	7
8	9	10	11	12	13	14
15	16	17	18	19	20	21
22	23	24	25	26	27	28
29	30	31				

Zone 1
- Plant autumn-flowering bulbs
- Plant potted shrubs, trees, groundcovers, vines, perennials, and biennials, and B&B shrubs, trees, groundcovers, and vines

- Transplant evergreens
- Prune groundcovers if needed; trim low-growing plants
- Train and prune vines
- Fertilize plants, if needed, for the last time until dormancy
- Keep the garden free of weeds
- Water as needed
- Spray with insecticides and fungicides if needed
- Remove faded flowers

Zone 2
- Plant autumn-flowering bulbs
- Plant potted shrubs, trees, groundcovers, vines, perennials, and biennials, and B&B shrubs, trees, groundcovers, and vines
- Transplant evergreens
- Prune groundcovers if needed; trim low-growing plants
- Train and prune vines
- Fertilize plants, if needed, for the last time until dormancy
- Keep the garden free of weeds
- Water as needed
- Spray with insecticides and fungicides if needed
- Remove faded flowers

Zone 3
- Plant autumn-flowering bulbs
- Plant potted shrubs, trees, groundcovers, vines, perennials, and biennials, and B&B shrubs, trees, groundcovers, and vines
- Transplant evergreens
- Prune groundcovers if needed; trim low-growing plants
- Train and prune vines
- Fertilize plants, if needed, for the last time until dormancy
- Keep the garden free of weeds
- Water as needed
- Spray with insecticides and fungicides if needed
- Remove faded flowers

Zone 4

- Plant autumn-flowering bulbs
- Plant potted shrubs, trees, groundcovers, vines, perennials, and biennials, and B&B shrubs, trees, groundcovers, and vines
- Prune groundcovers if needed; trim low-growing plants
- Train and prune vines
- Fertilize plants, if needed, for the last time until dormancy
- Keep the garden free of weeds
- Water as needed
- Spray with insecticides and fungicides if needed
- Remove faded flowers

Zone 5

- Order spring-flowering bulbs
- Plant autumn-flowering bulbs
- Plant potted shrubs, trees, groundcovers, vines, perennials, and biennials, and B&B shrubs, trees, groundcovers, and vines
- Prune groundcovers if needed; trim low-growing plants
- Train and prune vines
- Fertilize plants, if needed, for the last time until dormancy
- Keep the garden free of weeds
- Water as needed
- Spray with insecticides and fungicides if needed
- Remove faded flowers
- Pinch leggy plants
- Sow hardy and half-hardy annual seeds indoors or outdoors

Zone 6

- Order spring-flowering bulbs
- Plant autumn-flowering bulbs
- Plant potted shrubs, trees, groundcovers, vines, perennials, and biennials, and B&B shrubs, trees, groundcovers, and vines
- Prune groundcovers if needed; trim low-growing plants
- Train and prune vines

- Fertilize plants, if needed, for the last time until dormancy
- Keep the garden free of weeds
- Water as needed
- Spray with insecticides and fungicides if needed
- Remove faded flowers
- Pinch leggy plants
- Sow hardy and half-hardy annual seeds indoors or outdoors

Zone 7

- Order spring-flowering bulbs
- Plant autumn-flowering bulbs
- Plant potted shrubs, trees, groundcovers, vines, perennials, and biennials, and B&B trees, shrubs, groundcovers, and vines
- Prune groundcovers if needed; trim low-growing plants
- Train and prune vines
- Fertilize plants, if needed, for the last time until dormancy
- Keep the garden free of weeds
- Water as needed
- Spray with insecticides and fungicides if needed
- Remove faded flowers
- Pinch leggy plants
- Sow hardy and half-hardy annual seeds indoors or outdoors

Zone 8

- Order spring-flowering bulbs
- Plant autumn-flowering bulbs
- Plant potted shrubs, trees, groundcovers, vines, perennials, and biennials, and B&B shrubs, trees, groundcovers, and vines
- Prune groundcovers if needed; trim low-growing plants
- Train and prune vines
- Fertilize plants if needed
- Keep the garden free of weeds
- Water as needed
- Spray with insecticides and fungicides if needed

- Disbud flowering plants for larger blooms
- Remove faded flowers
- Pinch leggy plants
- Sow hardy and half-hardy annual seeds indoors or outdoors

Zone 9

- Plant autumn-flowering bulbs
- Plant potted shrubs, trees, groundcovers, vines, perennials, biennials, and B&B shrubs, trees, groundcovers, and vines
- Prune groundcovers if needed; trim low-growing plants
- Train and prune vines
- Fertilize plants if needed
- Keep the garden free of weeds
- Water as needed
- Spray with insecticides and fungicides if needed
- Pinch annuals and perennials if needed
- Disbud flowering plants for larger blooms
- Remove faded flowers
- Replace spent annual flowers
- Sow hardy and half-hardy annual seeds indoors or outdoors

Zone 10

- Plant autumn-flowering bulbs
- Plant potted shrubs, trees, groundcovers, vines, perennials, biennials, and B&B shrubs, trees, groundcovers, and vines
- Prune groundcovers if needed; trim low-growing plants
- Train and prune vines
- Fertilize plants if needed
- Keep the garden free of weeds
- Water as needed
- Spray with insecticides and fungicides if needed
- Pinch annuals and perennials if needed
- Disbud flowering plants for larger blooms

- Remove faded flowers
- Remove and replace spent annual flowers
- Sow hardy and half-hardy annual seeds indoors or outdoors

Zone 11
- Plant autumn-flowering bulbs
- Plant potted shrubs, trees, groundcovers, vines, perennials, biennials, and B&B shrubs, trees, groundcovers, and vines
- Prune groundcovers if needed; trim low-growing plants
- Train and prune vines
- Fertilize plants if needed
- Keep the garden free of weeds
- Water as needed
- Spray with insecticides and fungicides if needed
- Pinch annuals and perennials if needed
- Disbud flowering plants for larger blooms
- Remove faded flowers
- Remove and replace spent annual flowers
- Sow hardy and half-hardy annual seeds indoors or outdoors

SEPTEMBER

1	2	3	4	5	6	7
8	9	10	11	12	13	14
15	16	17	18	19	20	21
22	23	24	25	26	27	28
29	30					

Zone 1
- Prepare soil for autumn or spring planting
- Plant spring-flowering bulbs
- Dig and store tender bulbs
- Transplant deciduous shrubs and trees
- Clean up fallen leaves

- Cut back spent biennials and perennials
- Remove annuals killed by frost
- Sow seeds of woody plants and perennials needing stratification outdoors
- Apply winter protection
- Water as needed

Zone 2
- Prepare soil for autumn or spring planting
- Plant spring-flowering bulbs
- Dig and store tender bulbs
- Transplant deciduous shrubs and trees
- Rake and clean up fallen leaves
- Cut back spent biennials and perennials
- Remove annuals killed by frost
- Sow seeds of woody plants and perennials needing stratification outdoors
- Apply winter protection
- Water as needed

Zone 3
- Prepare soil for autumn or spring planting
- Plant spring-flowering bulbs
- Dig and store tender bulbs
- Transplant deciduous shrubs and trees
- Clean up fallen leaves
- Cut back spent biennials and perennials
- Remove annuals killed by frost
- Sow seeds of woody plants and perennials needing stratification outdoors
- Apply winter protection
- Water as needed

Zone 4
- Prepare soil for autumn or spring planting
- Plant spring-flowering bulbs
- Dig and store tender bulbs
- Transplant deciduous shrubs and trees

- Clean up fallen leaves
- Cut back spent biennials and perennials
- Remove annuals killed by frost
- Sow seeds of woody plants and perennials needing stratification outdoors
- Apply winter protection
- Water as needed

Zone 5
- Prepare soil for autumn or spring planting
- Plant spring-flowering bulbs
- Dig and store tender bulbs
- Keep the garden free of weeds
- Sow perennial and biennial seeds outdoors
- Divide and transplant perennials
- Transplant deciduous or evergreen shrubs and trees
- Sow seeds of woody plants and perennials needing stratification outdoors
- Apply winter protection
- Water as needed
- Remove faded flowers

Zone 6
- Prepare soil for autumn or spring planting
- Plant spring-flowering bulbs
- Keep the garden free of weeds
- Sow perennial and biennial seeds outdoors
- Divide and transplant perennials
- Trim plants if needed
- Train and tie vines if needed
- Transplant evergreens
- Water as needed
- Spray with insecticides and fungicides if needed
- Remove faded flowers

Zone 7
- Prepare soil for autumn or spring planting
- Plant spring-flowering bulbs

- Keep the garden free of weeds
- Sow perennial and biennial seeds outdoors
- Divide and transplant perennials
- Trim plants if needed
- Train and tie vines if needed
- Plant potted shrubs, trees, groundcovers, vines, and perennials, and B&B shrubs, trees, groundcovers, and vines
- Transplant evergreens
- Water as needed
- Spray with insecticides and fungicides if needed
- Remove faded flowers
- Take hardwood cuttings of woody plants for rooting

Zone 8

- Prepare soil for autumn or spring planting
- Plant spring-flowering bulbs
- Keep the garden free of weeds
- Sow perennial and biennial seeds outdoors
- Divide and transplant perennials
- Plant potted shrubs, trees, groundcovers, vines, and perennials, and B&B shrubs, trees, groundcovers, and vines
- Trim plants if needed
- Train and tie vines if needed
- Transplant evergreens
- Apply final fertilizer to plants until dormancy
- Water as needed
- Spray with insecticides and fungicides if needed
- Take hardwood cuttings of woody plants for rooting

Zone 9

- Keep the garden free of weeds
- Sow annual, perennial, and biennial seeds outdoors
- Divide and transplant perennials

- Plant potted shrubs, trees, groundcovers, vines, and perennials, and B&B shrubs, trees, groundcovers, and vines
- Trim plants if needed
- Train and tie vines if needed
- Transplant evergreens
- Water as needed
- Fertilize plants if needed
- Spray with insecticides and fungicides if needed
- Sow hardy and half-hardy annual seeds indoors
- Remove faded flowers
- Take hardwood cuttings of woody plants for rooting

Zone 10

- Keep the garden free of weeds
- Sow annual, perennial, and biennial seeds outdoors
- Divide and transplant perennials
- Plant potted shrubs, trees, groundcovers, vines, and perennials, and B&B shrubs, trees, groundcovers, and vines
- Trim plants if needed
- Train and tie vines if needed
- Transplant evergreens
- Water as needed
- Fertilize plants if needed
- Spray with insecticides and fungicides if needed
- Sow hardy and half-hardy annual seeds indoors
- Remove faded flowers

Zone 11

- Keep the garden free of weeds
- Sow annual, perennial, and biennial seeds outdoors
- Divide and transplant perennials
- Plant potted shrubs, trees, groundcovers, vines, and perennials, and B&B shrubs, trees, groundcovers, and vines
- Trim plants if needed
- Train and tie vines if needed

- Transplant evergreens
- Water as needed
- Fertilize plants if needed
- Spray with insecticides and fungicides if needed
- Sow hardy and half-hardy annual seeds indoors
- Remove faded flowers

OCTOBER						
1	2	3	4	5	6	7
8	9	10	11	12	13	14
15	16	17	18	19	20	21
22	23	24	25	26	27	28
29	30	31				

Zone 1

- Apply winter protection
- Apply dormant fertilizer to trees, shrubs, groundcovers, and vines
- Prune shade trees
- Rake leaves
- Spray evergreens with antidesiccant

Zone 2

- Apply winter protection
- Apply dormant fertilizer to trees, shrubs, groundcovers, and vines
- Prune shade trees
- Rake leaves
- Spray evergreens with antidesiccant

Zone 3

- Apply winter protection
- Apply dormant fertilizer to trees, shrubs, groundcovers, and vines
- Remove annuals killed by frost
- Prune shade trees
- Rake leaves
- Spray evergreens with antidesiccant

Zone 4
- Apply winter protection
- Apply dormant fertilizer to trees, shrubs, groundcovers, and vines
- Remove annuals killed by frost
- Plant very hardy annuals
- Prune shade trees
- Rake leaves
- Spray evergreens with antidesiccant

Zone 5
- Prepare soil for spring planting
- Water as needed
- Remove annuals killed by frost
- Plant hardy annuals
- Transplant deciduous trees and shrubs, and groundcovers
- Prune shade trees
- Rake leaves

Zone 6
- Prepare soil for spring planting
- Keep the garden free of weeds
- Plant potted perennials and biennials
- Plant bare-root trees, shrubs, groundcovers, and vines
- Divide and transplant perennials and groundcovers
- Transplant deciduous trees and shrubs
- Plant hardy annuals
- Prune shade trees
- Rake leaves
- Plant spring-flowering bulbs
- Dig and store tender bulbs
- Water plants if needed, especially evergreens
- Sow seeds of woody plants and perennials that need stratification outdoors

Zone 7
- Prepare soil for spring planting
- Keep the garden free of weeds

- Plant potted perennials, biennials, trees, shrubs, groundcovers, and vines, and B&B trees, shrubs, groundcovers and vines
- Divide and transplant perennials and groundcovers
- Plant bare-root shrubs, trees, groundcovers, and vines
- Transplant deciduous trees and shrubs
- Plant hardy annuals
- Water as needed
- Spray with insecticides and fungicides if needed
- Prune groundcovers if needed
- Train and prune vines if needed
- Plant spring-flowering bulbs
- Rake leaves
- Sow seeds of woody plants and perennials that need stratification outdoors
- Take hardwood cuttings for rooting

Zone 8
- Prepare soil for autumn or spring planting
- Keep the garden free of weeds
- Plant potted perennials, biennials, shrubs, trees, groundcovers, and vines, and B&B shrubs, trees, groundcovers, and vines
- Plant bare-root shrubs, trees, groundcovers, and vines
- Divide and transplant perennials and groundcovers
- Transplant deciduous trees and shrubs
- Plant hardy annuals
- Water as needed
- Spray with insecticides and fungicides if needed
- Prune groundcovers if needed
- Train and prune vines if needed
- Remove and replace spent annual plants
- Plant spring-flowering bulbs

- Rake leaves
- Take hardwood cuttings for rooting

Zone 9
- Prepare soil for autumn or spring planting
- Keep the garden free of weeds
- Plant potted perennials, biennials, shrubs, trees, groundcovers, and vines, and B&B shrubs, trees, groundcovers, and vines
- Plant bare-root shrubs, trees, groundcovers, and vines
- Divide and transplant perennials and groundcovers
- Transplant deciduous trees and shrubs
- Plant hardy annuals
- Water as needed
- Spray with insecticides and fungicides if needed
- Prune groundcovers if needed
- Train and prune vines if needed
- Fertilize the garden as needed
- Replace spent annuals
- Plant spring-flowering bulbs
- Take hardwood cuttings for rooting

Zone 10
- Prepare soil for autumn or spring planting
- Keep the garden free of weeds
- Plant potted perennials, biennials, shrubs, trees, groundcovers, and vines, and B&B shrubs, trees, groundcovers, and vines
- Plant bare-root shrubs, trees, groundcovers, and vines
- Divide and transplant perennials and groundcovers
- Transplant deciduous trees and shrubs
- Water as needed
- Spray with insecticides and fungicides if needed

- Prune groundcovers if needed
- Train and prune vines if needed
- Fertilize the garden if needed
- Replace spent annuals

Zone 11

- Prepare soil for autumn or spring planting
- Keep the garden free of weeds
- Plant potted perennials, biennials, shrubs, trees, groundcovers, and vines, and B&B shrubs, trees, groundcovers, and vines
- Plant bare-root shrubs, trees, groundcovers, and vines
- Divide and transplant perennials and groundcovers
- Transplant deciduous trees and shrubs
- Water as needed
- Spray with insecticides and fungicides if needed
- Prune groundcovers if needed
- Train and prune vines if needed
- Fertilize the garden if needed
- Replace spent annuals

NOVEMBER

1	2	3	4	5	6	7
8	9	10	11	12	13	14
15	16	17	18	19	20	21
22	23	24	25	26	27	28
29	30					

Zone 1

- Check winter protection; add more if necessary
- Order plants for spring planting
- Spray evergreens with antidesiccant

Zone 2

- Check winter protection; add more if necessary
- Order plants for spring planting
- Spray evergreens with antidesiccant

Zone 3

- Check winter protection; add more if necessary
- Order plants for spring planting
- Spray evergreens with antidesiccant

Zone 4

- Check winter protection; add more if necessary
- Order plants for spring planting
- Spray evergreens with antidesiccant

Zone 5

- Check winter protection; add more if necessary
- Order plants for spring planting
- Apply dormant fertilizer to trees, shrubs, groundcovers, and vines
- Prune shade trees
- Cut back tops of spent perennials
- Remove annuals killed by frost
- Plant and mulch very hardy annuals
- Rake leaves
- Spray evergreens with antidesiccant

Zone 6

- Order plants for spring planting
- Apply dormant fertilizer to trees, shrubs, groundcovers, and vines
- Prune shade trees
- Apply winter protection
- Plant very hardy annuals
- Cut back tops of spent perennials
- Remove annuals killed by frost
- Rake leaves
- Prepare soil for autumn or spring planting
- Plant bare-root perennials, trees, shrubs, groundcovers, and vines
- Plant spring-flowering bulbs
- Dig and store tender bulbs

- Spray evergreens with antidesiccant
- Water evergreens if needed

Zone 7

- Order plants for spring planting
- Apply winter protection
- Cut back tops of spent perennials
- Plant and mulch hardy annuals
- Remove annuals killed by frost
- Rake leaves
- Prepare soil for autumn or spring planting
- Plant bare-root perennials, trees, shrubs, groundcovers, and vines
- Apply dormant fertilizer to trees, shrubs, groundcovers, and vines
- Prune shade trees
- Plant spring-flowering bulbs
- Dig and store tender bulbs
- Spray evergreens with antidesiccant
- Water evergreens if needed

Zone 8

- Order plants for spring planting
- Apply winter protection
- Cut back tops of spent perennials
- Remove annuals killed by frost
- Plant and mulch hardy annuals
- Rake leaves
- Prepare soil for autumn or spring planting
- Plant potted or bare-root biennials, perennials, trees, shrubs, groundcovers, vines, and B&B shrubs, trees, groundcovers, and vines
- Transplant deciduous shrubs and trees
- Prune shade trees
- Plant spring-flowering bulbs
- Sow biennial and perennial seeds outdoors
- Sow seeds of woody plants outdoors

- Divide and transplant perennials and groundcovers
- Dig and store tender bulbs
- Water plants, if needed, especially evergreens

Zone 9

- Order plants for spring planting
- Cut back tops of spent perennials
- Remove annuals killed by frost
- Plant hardy and half-hardy annual seeds and transplant outdoors
- Rake leaves
- Prepare soil for autumn or spring planting
- Plant potted or bare-root biennials, perennials, trees, shrubs, groundcovers, vines, and B&B shrubs, trees, groundcovers, and vines
- Plant spring-flowering bulbs
- Sow biennial and perennial seeds outdoors
- Sow seeds of woody plants outdoors
- Divide and transplant perennials and groundcovers
- Prune shade trees
- Prune groundcovers if needed
- Train and prune vines if needed
- Dig and store tender bulbs
- Fertilize plants if needed
- Water plants if needed
- Withhold water from established plants to induce dormancy
- Spray with insecticides and fungicides if needed
- Keep the garden free of weeds

Zone 10

- Plant tender bulbs
- Replace spent annuals
- Order plants for spring planting
- Cut back tops of spent perennials
- Plant seeds and transplants outdoors

- Rake leaves
- Prepare soil for autumn or spring planting
- Plant potted or bare-root biennials, perennials, trees, shrubs, groundcovers, vines, and B&B shrubs, trees, groundcovers, and vines
- Sow biennial and perennial seeds outdoors
- Sow seeds of woody plants outdoors
- Divide and transplant perennials and groundcovers
- Prune shade trees
- Prune groundcovers if needed
- Train and prune vines if needed
- Fertilize plants if needed
- Water plants if needed
- Withhold water from established plants to induce dormancy
- Spray with insecticides and fungicides if needed
- Keep the garden free of weeds

Zone 11

- Plant tender bulbs
- Replace spent annuals
- Order plants for spring planting
- Cut back tops of spent perennials
- Plant seeds and transplants outdoors
- Rake leaves
- Prepare soil for autumn or spring planting
- Plant potted or bare-root biennials, perennials, trees, shrubs, groundcovers, vines, and B&B shrubs, trees, groundcovers, and vines
- Sow biennial and perennial seeds outdoors
- Sow seeds of woody plants outdoors
- Divide and transplant perennials and groundcovers
- Prune shade trees
- Prune groundcovers if needed

- Train and prune vines if needed
- Fertilize plants if needed
- Water plants if needed
- Withhold water from established plants to induce dormancy
- Spray with insecticides and fungicides if needed
- Keep the garden free of weeds

DECEMBER

1	2	3	4	5	6	7
8	9	10	11	12	13	14
15	16	17	18	19	20	21
22	23	24	25	26	27	28
29	30	31				

Zone 1

- Order plants and seeds for spring
- Remove snow and ice from evergreens

Zone 2

- Order plants and seeds for spring
- Remove snow and ice from evergreens

Zone 3

- Order plants and seeds for spring
- Remove snow and ice from evergreens

Zone 4

- Order plants and seeds for spring
- Remove snow and ice from evergreens

Zone 5

- Order plants and seeds for spring
- Remove snow and ice from evergreens

Zone 6
- Order plants and seeds for spring
- Remove snow and ice from evergreens

Zone 7
- Order plants and seeds for spring
- Prune shade trees
- Remove snow and ice from evergreens
- Spray evergreens with antidesiccant

Zone 8
- Order plants and seeds for spring
- Prepare soil for planting
- Plant potted or bare-root perennials, shrubs, trees, groundcovers, and vines, and B&B shrubs, trees, groundcovers, and vines
- Divide and transplant perennials and groundcovers
- Transplant shrubs and trees
- Prune shade trees
- Apply dormant fertilizer to trees, shrubs, groundcovers, and vines
- Apply winter protection
- Sow seeds of hardy annuals indoors
- Sow tender annual seeds indoors that require 12 weeks or more
- Spray evergreens with antidesiccant

Zone 9
- Refrigerate hardy bulbs that require chilling
- Order plants and seeds for spring
- Prepare soil for planting

- Plant potted or bare-root perennials, shrubs, trees, groundcovers, and vines, and B&B shrubs, trees, groundcovers, and vines
- Divide and transplant perennials and groundcovers
- Remove annuals killed by frost
- Transplant shrubs and trees
- Prune shade trees
- Prune groundcovers if needed
- Train and prune vines if needed
- Fertilize plants if needed
- Sow seeds of hardy annuals indoors
- Sow biennial and perennial seeds indoors or outdoors
- Sow seeds of tender annuals that require 12 weeks or more indoors
- Plant hardy and half-hardy seeds and transplants outdoors
- Water as needed
- Spray with insecticides and pesticides if needed

Zone 10
- Plant tender bulbs
- Refrigerate hardy bulbs that require chilling
- Order plants and seeds for spring
- Prepare soil for planting
- Plant potted or bare-root perennials, shrubs, trees, groundcovers, and vines, and B&B shrubs, trees, groundcovers, and vines
- Divide and transplant perennial herbs and flowers and groundcovers
- Transplant shrubs and trees
- Prune shade trees
- Prune groundcovers if needed
- Train and prune vines if needed
- Fertilize plants if needed

- Keep the garden free of weeds
- Sow seeds of hardy annuals indoors
- Sow biennial and perennial seeds indoors or outdoors
- Sow seeds of tender annuals indoors
- Plant hardy and half-hardy seeds and transplants outdoors
- Water plants if needed
- Spray with insecticides and pesticides if needed

Zone 11
- Plant tender bulbs
- Refrigerate hardy bulbs that require chilling
- Order plants and seeds for spring
- Prepare soil for planting
- Plant potted or bare-root perennials, shrubs, trees, groundcovers, and vines, and B&B shrubs, trees, groundcovers, and vines
- Divide and transplant perennials and groundcovers
- Transplant shrubs and trees
- Prune shade trees
- Prune groundcovers if needed
- Train and prune vines if needed
- Fertilize plants if needed
- Keep the garden free of weeds
- Sow seeds of hardy annuals indoors
- Sow biennial and perennial seeds indoors or outdoors
- Sow seeds of tender annuals indoors
- Plant hardy and half-hardy seeds and transplants outdoors
- Water plants if needed
- Spray with insecticides and pesticides if needed

About
the
Author

Derek Fell is a writer and photographer who specializes in gardening, with an emphasis on step-by-step gardening concepts and garden design. He lives in Bucks County, Pennsylvania, at historic Cedaridge Farm, Tinicum Township, where he cultivates extensive award-winning flower and vegetable gardens that have been featured in *Architectural Digest, Garden Design, Beautiful Gardens, Gardens Illustrated, American Nurseryman,* and *Mid-Atlantic Country* magazines. Born and educated in England, he first worked for seven years with Europe's largest seed company, then moved to Pennsylvania in 1964 to work for Burpee Seeds as their catalog manager, a position he held for six years before taking on duties as executive director of the All-America Selections (the national seed trials) and the National Garden Bureau (an information office sponsored by the American seed industry). Now the author of more than fifty garden books and calendars, he has traveled widely throughout North America, also documenting gardens in Europe, Africa, New Zealand, and Asia. His most recent books are *Herb Gardening with Derek Fell, Bulb Gardening with Derek Fell,* and *Secrets of Monet's Garden*

A frequent contributor to *Architectural Digest* and *Woman's Day* magazines, Derek Fell is the winner of more awards from the Garden Writers Association of America than any other garden writer. He also worked as a consultant on gardening to the White House during the Ford Administration.

Wall calendars, greeting cards, and art posters featuring Derek Fell's photography are published worldwide. He has lectured on photography and the gardens of the great Impressionist painters at numerous art museums, including the Smithsonian Institution in Washington, D.C.; the Philadelphia Museum of Art and the Barnes Foundation, Philadelphia; and the Denver Art Museum, Colorado. He is also host of a regular garden show for the QVC cable television shopping channel, entitled *Step-by-Step Gardening,* which is plugged into fifty million homes.

Fell's highly acclaimed *Step-by-Step Gardening* mail-order perennial plant catalogs for Spring Hill Nurseries (North America's largest mail-order nursery) reach an audience of home gardeners estimated to be more than three million in spring and autumn. He is a former president of the Hobby Greenhouse Association, a former director of the Garden Writers Association of America, the president of the International Test Gardeners Association, and a cofounder of the American Gardening Association.

A complete list of published works follows.

Books by Derek Fell

(An asterisk indicates coauthorship.)

The White House Vegetable Garden. 1976, Exposition.

House Plants for Fun & Profit. 1978, Bookworm.

How to Photograph Flowers, Plants, & Landscapes. 1980, HP Books.

Vegetables: How to Select, Grow, and Enjoy. 1982, HP Books.

Annuals: How to Select, Grow, and Enjoy. 1983, HP Books.

Deerfield: An American Garden Through Four Seasons. 1986, Pidcock Press.

Trees & Shrubs. 1986, HP Books.

Garden Accents. 1987, Henry Holt. (*Inspired Garden* in the United Kingdom)

*Discover Anguilla. 1988, Caribbean Concepts.

*Home Landscaping. 1988, Simon & Schuster.

The One-Minute Gardener. 1988, Running Press.

A Kid's First Gardening Book. 1989, Running Press.

*Three Year Garden Journal. 1989, Starwood.

*Ornamental Grass Gardening. 1989, HP Books.

*The Complete Garden Planning Manual. 1989, HP Books.

The Essential Gardener. 1990, Crown.

Essential Roses. 1990, Crown.

Essential Annuals. 1990, Crown.

Essential Bulbs. 1990, Crown.

Essential Perennials. 1990, Crown.

Essential Shrubs. 1990, Crown.

The Easiest Flower to Grow. 1990, Ortho.

*550 Home Landscaping Ideas. 1991, Simon & Schuster.

Renoir's Garden. 1991, Simon & Schuster.

Beautiful Bucks County. 1991, Cedaridge.

*The Encyclopedia of Ornamental Grasses. 1992, Smithmark.

The Encyclopedia of Flowers. 1993, Smithmark.

*550 Perennial Garden Ideas. 1993, Simon & Schuster.

The Impressionist Garden. 1994, Crown.

*Practical Gardening. 1995, Friedman/Fairfax.

*Gardens of Philadelphia & the Delaware Valley. 1995, Temple University Press.

The Pennsylvania Gardener. 1995, Camino Books.

In the Garden with Derek. 1995, Camino Books.

*Glorious Flowers. 1996, Friedman/Fairfax.

Perennial Gardening with Derek Fell. 1996, Friedman/Fairfax.

Vegetable Gardening with Derek Fell. 1996, Friedman/Fairfax

Derek Fell's Handy Garden Guides: Annuals. 1996, Friedman/Fairfax.

Derek Fell's Handy Garden Guides: Perennials. 1996, Friedman/Fairfax.

Derek Fell's Handy Garden Guides: Roses. 1996, Friedman/Fairfax.

Derek Fell's Handy Garden Guides: Bulbs. 1996, Friedman/Fairfax.

Herb Gardening with Derek Fell. 1997, Friedman/Fairfax.

Bulb Gardening with Derek Fell. 1997, Friedman/Fairfax.

Secrets of Monet's Garden. 1997, Friedman/Fairfax.

Calendars

Great Gardens (Portal)

Monet's Garden (Portal)

The Impressionist Garden (Portal)

The Gardening Year (Portal)

Perennials (Starwood)

Flowering Shrubs (Starwood)

Flowering Bulbs (Starwood)

Northeast Gardens Calendar (Starwood)

Mid-Atlantic Gardens Calendar (Starwood)

Southern Gardens Calendar (Starwood)

California Gardens Calendar (Starwood)

Pacific Northwest Gardens Calendar (Starwood)

Art Posters

Deerfield Garden (Portal)

Spring Garden (Portal)

Monet's Bridge (Portal)

Sources

Plants for shade gardens are available from many sources, especially from mail-order perennial plant specialists such as Spring Hill Nurseries, 110 W. Elm Street, Tipp City, OH 45371. The number of mail-order sources is too great to list every one, so the following list focuses on specialists of particular plant groups suitable for shade. For a larger list of sources, refer to the classified sections of monthly garden magazines, where many plant sources are advertised.

Azaleas
Carlson's Gardens
Box 305
South Salem, NY 10590

Begonias
Dutch Gardens
Box 200
Adelphia, NJ 07710

Caladiums
Caladium World
Box 129
Sebring, FL 33871

Camellias
Nuccio Nurseries
Box 6160
Altadena, CA 91001

Daffodils
The Daffodil Mart
Box 794
Gloucester, VA 23061

Ferns
Foliage Gardens
2003 128th Avenue SE
Bellevue, WA 98005

Hellebores
Piccadilly Farm
1971 Whippoorwill Road
Bishop, GA 30621

Hostas
Klehm Nursery
Box 197
South Barrington, IL
60010

Insect-Eating Plants
Peter Paul's Nursery
RD 2
Canandaigua, NY 14424

Lilies
B&D Lilies
330 P Street
Port Townsend, WA
98368

Peonies
Gilbert H. Wild & Son
Box 338
Sarcoxie, MO 64862

Primulas
Barnhaven Primroses
Langerhouad
22420 Plouzelambre
France
(This company sells seed direct and provides a list of North American sources for plants.)

Wildflowers
Gardens of the Blue Ridge
Box 10
Pineola, NC 28662

Australia

Country Farm Perennials
RSD Laings Road
Nayook VIC 3821

Cox's Nursery
RMB 216 Oaks Road
Thrilmere NSW 2572

Honeysuckle Cottage
   Nursery
Lot 35 Bowen Mountain
Road
Bowen Mountain via
Grosevale NSW 2753

Swan Bros Pty Ltd
490 Galston Road
Dural NSW 2158

Canada

Corn Hill Nursery Ltd.
RR 5
Petitcodiac NB EOA
2HO

Ferncliff Gardens
SS 1
Mission, British Columbia
V2V 5V6

McFayden Seed Co. Ltd.
Box 1800
Brandon, Manitoba
R7A 6N4

Stirling Perennials
RR 1
Morpeth, Ontario
N0P 1X0

PLANT HARDINESS ZONES

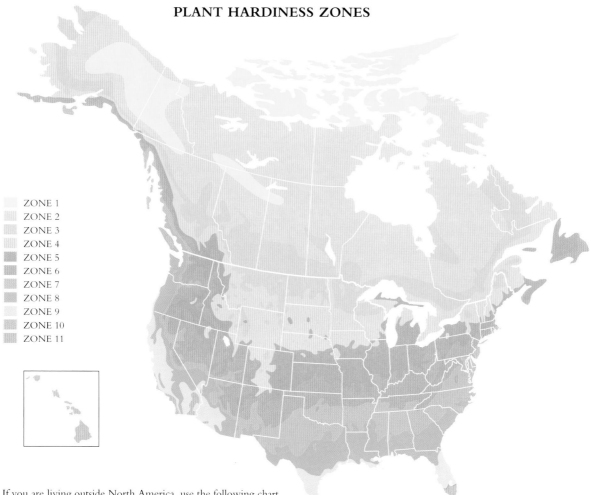

ZONE 1
ZONE 2
ZONE 3
ZONE 4
ZONE 5
ZONE 6
ZONE 7
ZONE 8
ZONE 9
ZONE 10
ZONE 11

If you are living outside North America, use the following chart
to determine your plant hardiness zone.

Range of Average Annual MinimumTemperatures for Each Zone

	Farenheit (°F)	Celsius (°C)
ZONE 1	Below –50°	Below –45.6°
ZONE 2	–50° to –40°	–45.6° to –40°
ZONE 3	–40° to –30°	–40° to –34.4°
ZONE 4	–30° to –20°	–34.4° to –28.9°
ZONE 5	–20° to –10°	–28.9° to –23.3°
ZONE 6	–10° to 0°	–23.3° to –17.8°
ZONE 7	0° to 10°	–17.8° to –12.2°
ZONE 8	10° to 20°	–12.2° to –6.7°
ZONE 9	20° to 30°	–6.7° to –1.1°
ZONE 10	30° to 40°	–1.1° to 4.4°
ZONE 11	Above 40°	Above 4.4°

Index